To Bob

from

HOW TO
RECESSION
PROOF

YOUR
BUSINESS

André Larabie, CBC, CMC, MBA
& Dane Kress, CBC, BEd.

HOW TO
RECESSION PROOF
YOUR BUSINESS

By André Larabie
&
Dane Kress

Published by: André Larabie

6 Appaloosa Dr. Ottawa (Kanata, Ont) K2M 1N6, Canada

e-mail: Andre@AndreLarabie.com

Website: www.AndreLarabie.com

Legal Notices

ISBN-13: 978-1494955526

ISBN-10: 1494955520

CONTENTS

Introduction

We decided to write this book because the world economy is in such terrible shape and getting worse daily. Businesses all over the world are struggling, and the following question arises:

What could you do to prepare your business for future economic calamity?

For some businesses it is already too late; the time to prepare has passed; for others, there is still time. They have the resources to weather the storm and take the necessary steps to strengthen their business, even in these dire economic times. If they do have the required resources, it is important that they take the proper steps to stabilize.

We are business consultants and coaches, and we work with clients who are either (1) already in debt beyond their means, (2) being sued for non-payment of debt, or

(3) in need of a company turnaround specialist who can assist them with problems in every department in their business.

The stock market seems to be recovering after taking epic tumbles almost every week, and we (along with many reputable economists) believe there is yet another recession on the horizon. It is becoming apparent to everyone that America can no longer live on credit, and neither should you (personally or in your business). The US government is trying to keep the US dollar strong, but with the debt level at an all-time high, it's going to be difficult to avoid a second recession, and this may lead to a huge economic meltdown. The real estate bubble has already taken down millions of homeowners, and with the possibility of a double-dip recession looming large, many other homeowners will not be able to pay their mortgages, and the bank will soon foreclose on them.

Businesses are filing for bankruptcy by the thousands each month, and although this trend is expected to slow, if the US government does not do a better job of managing public finances, a second recession—with further economic calamity—is a near certainty.

This book will assist any business owner in taking the steps necessary to recession-proof their organization. The general approach is to first take an inventory of what they have and what they don't have; second, determine what they need; and third, come up with a plan to turn the business around and survive a potential recession. We will provide details on how to create a vision for your business, how to create a mission statement, how to increase your sales and reduce your expenses, and how to obtain tools that will allow you to use the Internet to grow your business. We will also show you how to provide your employees with a job description that outlines clear objectives. We will instruct you on the techniques you can use to negotiate with your creditors and make them an offer they can't refuse, and show you how to put together a turnaround plan that will provide you with some assurance that you can survive this downturn in the economy.

For the next few hours—or days if you choose to really study this book—you will discover some of the most important techniques to grow your business and make it prosper. And above all, these techniques will work for anyone and everyone.

Marketing Methods That Produce Top Results

All of the information in this book is tried and true, battle hardened, and tested. All of it is easy to follow and apply, and these strategies and ideas are going to help you grow your business far beyond what you could have ever imagined.

We will present cutting-edge techniques that will allow you to leverage the latest technology to globalize your business. These techniques are available to anyone, yet hardly any business owners are savvy enough to implement all of them at once. For example, although some business owners have started using email marketing and List management techniques, hardly any of them also implement article marketing or social media methods. The key concept here is that times have changed and it is no longer adequate to have only *local* streams of revenue.

If you want to endure the current recession and prepare your business to survive the next downturn, study this book and understand how to globalize your business. If you apply these key concepts—as we have helped others to do—you will succeed in the same fashion they have. These methods are proven and if you study this book closely, the concepts will be easy to follow and understand.

So no matter how bad your current situation is, don't give up hope. Many business owners are facing similar negative scenarios. A common—and very natural—reaction is to ignore the problems, but sooner or later, you will need to face the reality of your predicament. We are going to provide you with all the necessary information and methods to insure that you are able to face the difficulties head-on and make it through these tough times ahead.

Now let's get to work.

1

Why Recession-Proof
Your Business

Global Economic Outlook

By now, most people are starting to realize that the recent recession (in 2008-2013) is like no other recession in history. The economic conditions are different this time, and we are clearly not going to bounce back as easily as we have after other downturns. In fact, many economists are indicating that we are headed into—or are already in—one of those dreaded double-dip recessions. These types of fears can send the stock market into a breathtaking tailspin.

To make matters worse, the US government continues to borrow money like never before. The price of gold is skyrocketing because Uncle Sam is fiendishly printing money to pay interest on the debt, and this is making the value of the US dollar drop like a ton of lead.

In theory, the devalued US dollar should make stocks

rise, since like gold, securities are a viable investment alternative to cash. For this reason, dollars are flowing into gold and stock market securities. While the price of gold initially rose up like a rocket ship and then pulled back some, the stock market continues to rise. This has to be one of the most insidious signs of serious trouble brewing since the devalued dollar is now propping up the stock market. The economy seems dismal even though the stock market rises. This counter-intuitive result seems to indicate that a massive crash may be in the near future.

The United States is sort of like the proverbial boiled frog, floating in the warming water as the fire heats the economic pan—the excessive debt, the endless spending, the increasingly obese government, the skyrocketing prices, the seemingly negligent politicians. The poor US "frog" is being lulled into complacency and will not realize it is time to jump out until she is cooked to the core!

If you doubt this, take a look at the rising prices in your local grocery store (and many other places). While some items are visibly increasing in price, others seem to remain the same; however, upon closer inspection, you will notice something insidious: as the value of the dollar tumbles at a dizzying rate, manufacturers avoid bumping up the price tag by making the package smaller.

The water temperature is rising...

According to a recent New York Times article[1] titled *Food Inflation Kept Hidden in Tinier Bags*, Nabisco foods has reduced the cracker count in their flagship saltine cracker product by roughly 15% while keeping the price fixed. Countless other manufacturers are resorting to the

[1] www.nytimes.com, March 29, 2011.

same shenanigans, and this phenomenon is not limited to personal products. Many business owners are also feeling the effects of this stealthy, cost-cutting sleight-of-hand.

In fact, we are witnessing the results of the failed borrowing strategy advocated by purveyors of Keynesian Economics. After the spectacular US financial meltdown in 2008, Americans filled their senate, congress, and presidency with tax-and-spend democrats who advocate huge government programs—a philosophy underscored by the following general strategy:

In times of severe economic crisis, the government should borrow money, spend more than they borrow, and then borrow yet more money to boost demand and generate "growth."

To implement their philosophy, they passed a stimulus bill that cost US taxpayers nearly $800 billion. They wrongly believed that an artificial increase in consumer demand would prompt the economy into recovery—as if another injection of heroin would solve the problems of a desperate heroin addict.

Hardly!

Now it has become painfully clear that this quick fix did not work. Although the unemployment rate appears to be dropping after a brief flirt with 10%—epic levels by any measurement—this number does not take into account the millions of potential workers who have simply given up all hope and quit looking. It also does reflect the massive increase in public sector workers hired to support the massive government expansion embodied by ObamaCare and other socialistic programs that essentially prey on private business. The more bloated the government grows in proportion to the shrinking private sector, the more meaningless these economic indicators are. This colossal economic failure is now like a fire raging out of control.

And what are the politicians doing about it?

They are printing more US dollars! This is like a waterless fool throwing gasoline on a fire hoping to put it out! This picture looks (and sounds) gloomy, and it really is.

In reality, American politicians are making a fundamental mistake: They are not recognizing that a significant change has taken place in the world. The Internet has transformed the playing field. It is no longer a local, regional, or national economy; rather, it is a GLOBAL ECONOMY.

We put that in capitals because not only is this fundamental change responsible for the recent economic decline of America. It also offers a *solution* to the problem.

If they would only recognize this global change has taken place, maybe they could implement NEW economic policies that would successfully transport our "last-century" economy into this new world of globalization. To succeed, the politicians must take this fundamental transformation into account because the old fixes no longer work.

The old fixes will no longer work!

But this book has not been written to help the US Government understand why their country is failing and how they can fix their declining economy; rather, it is intended for the business owner who wishes to recession-proof their business. The concepts we present herein show the reader how to stabilize their business and prepare it to weather any future recessions.

Why would a business owner want to do this?

The answer is simple...

If you do not recession-proof your business, there is a very good chance you will eventually go out of business.

Just like the US Government appears to be doing now...

Why will you go out of business?

Because, as mentioned above, the playing field has undergone a huge transformation. We are no longer playing on a local, regional, or national playing field; rather, we are now playing a *global* game of business, and those who continue to ignore this will eventually fail—just like the US is failing.

The signs are everywhere.

A Fundamental Change Has Occurred

Let's consider a very high profile sign of a system that no longer works in this global economy. If we consider the recent events in the state of Wisconsin—in particular those efforts to make fundamental changes that undermine the political stranglehold labor unions have on local governments, we can see a perfect example. Traditionally, labor unions ignore competitive forces and impose unrealistic costs on employers. With great fanfare in Wisconsin, union leaders held on to collective bargaining powers that may have made sense in the older

21

economy of last century, but now they are outdated.

These bargaining powers give unions the ability to keep salaries and benefits artificially high—in defiance of the free market. For many years, unions were allowed to operate in the shadows, extracting these unrealistic resources from their employers—and indirectly from the unwary taxpayers. But now, with resources dwindling due to global competitive pressures—due to the paradigm shift we are experiencing—the entire economy is under pressure, and these absurd union tactics no longer go unnoticed. This is an indirect sign that *global* pressures are having a *local* impact.

Another sign is simple and highly visible: jobs are going overseas. This needs no explanation; everyone knows it is happening and the statistics bear it out. People in the US are losing their jobs and those jobs are being filled by foreigners. Companies are shutting down US plants and moving them overseas. Again, we have external pressures, a new playing field, a global marketplace.

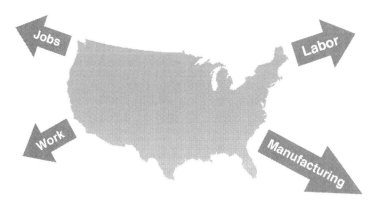

Another case in point is the bankruptcy of Borders

Book Stores and the closing of all their outlets. This is a perfect example of the new economy at work. The Internet is transforming the way we communicate, and the way we must do business. Borders failed to recognize that and they are paying the price.

If you fail to recognize the tremendous groundswell of these changes, and you continue to operate your business like nothing has changed, you will end up like the proverbial blind man, stumbling into a busy intersection. The landscape has changed and you need to take advantage of that change rather than ignore it.

Let's consider another topic that will underscore the need to make changes in your business: *The Yellow Pages.*

Just 10 years ago, the Yellow Pages were a viable method of advertising and one of the best ways for most businesses to communicate their information to prospective clients. In fact, advertising in the Yellow Pages was a must for *every* business back then. If your company was not listed there, potential customers might wrongly assume that you were new in town or not viable as a business—if they could even find you at all.

You simply had to advertise in the Yellow Pages, but now this is no longer true. Other options are evolving.

The demise of the Yellow Pages is yet another clear sign of the fundamental paradigm shift occurring around us. Instead of listing your business in the Yellow Pages, where can you list it now? Actually, there is not one clear advertising method that has evolved enough to replace the Yellow Pages; rather, there are a multitude of replacements. Craigslist and Google are two of the more prominent ones.

Instead of searching out a phone booth with a tattered phone book, pages blowing in the wind, new prospective clients lift their cell phone and verbally request a phone number. Voice recognition programs handle the rest. No need to waste trees communicating to customers with an obsolete yellow reference book.

What we are talking about is a new way to communicate with clients. We no longer advertise in the Yellow Pages. We no longer advertise in the newspaper. Sure, we can still do those things, but they are no longer adequate.

Why?

Because many prospective clients no longer communicate using those old funky methods. Traditionally, communicating with clients was more of a *one-way street* so it was OK to put your information in the phone book and wait for clients to arrive at your doorstep.

In the good old days, you placed an advertisement in the Yellow Pages or the newspaper; you rented a roadside sign; you printed a thousand brochures and dropped them off at the post office. Oh, by the way, in case you haven't heard yet, the US Postal Service is also going out of business!

Why?

Simply because they also failed to recognize that things have changed. Like the increasingly defunct US Government, the good old USPS continues to operate in the last century. Like the labor union leaders, they continue their reliance on tactics that worked decades ago.

Now the process of communicating with clients is

more *bidirectional*, more *real-time*. Consider social media, Facebook in particular. Many companies are creating a Facebook presence. With social media, businesses communicate more with their customers in real time and the interaction is more dynamic. Another example of a viable social media tool is Twitter. With a Twitter account, business managers can inform clients, and potential clients, of new products and services *immediately*.

They no longer have to print the product announcement and take it to the post office to have it sent to their clients. They don't have to spend months working on that new print catalog. Now they upload it to their website and post links to it on Facebook, or they Twitter it out into cyberland—to thousands of customers, all at the speed of electricity. If you fail to recognize these fundamental changes you will go out of business!

Just like the unions, you will eventually be rooted out of your deep dark hole. Just like the failed stimulus package, your revenues will disappear into the bottomless pit of "last century." Just like the Yellow Pages, you will become obsolete. Just like the US Postal Service, you will eventually declare bankruptcy (in some form or other). Just like the sad owners of Borders Book Stores, you will be forced into retirement.

Instead of fighting this change—and the new technology ushering it in—you need to *embrace* it. Be proactive! Utilize the technology that is now available to empower your business.

This technology and the new marketing techniques

it supports (think customer communication methods) will allow you to recession-proof your business. By understanding and utilizing the methods we present in this book, both new ones and some of the basic business methods that have not changed, you can stabilize your company and protect it from future failure.

After researching other books on these topics, we finally concluded that no authors (besides us, with this book) have got it right. Many books present only some of the new methods or some of the old methods. We contend that neither approach will work if you only use that approach alone. Rather, to succeed you must utilize a *combination* of strategies to stabilize and prepare your business for the global economy.

These new methods we are referring to are those techniques that deal with social media or online marketing, among others, presented herein, with the older methods being debt reduction, business growth, and business turnaround topics.

The government will not save you. You cannot afford to sit idly by, as the US Postal Service has done, waiting for the Uncle Sam to bail you out. Do you think you can fly to Washington, DC to speak in front of a US Congressional committee to complain about your problems and hope they will reach into the taxpayers' pockets to give you a handout so you can continue operating your bloated failure of a company?

Hardly!

Do you think you can act like the unions and go on "strike" to convince your clients—with scare tactics and bullying—to continue doing business with you, continue giving you unrealistic gobs of money, even though you operate with last-century methods?

Hardly!

Do you think you can advertise only in the Yellow Pages and the newspaper and your company will continue to grow at the same rate as it has in the past?

Hardly!

What will you do when you print up 10,000 brochures and drive down the post office only to find the doors locked with a chain and padlock, the building dark inside?

It is getting late in the game, but not too late.

You can still take action to stabilize your business and prepare for the inevitable future that is unfolding around us. Maybe, like the US Government with their defunct stimulus program, you have tried various actions to revitalize your business. Maybe you did a newspaper advertising blitz or a frantic radio campaign—maybe you too flushed valuable resources down the drain, only to realize they no longer work.

Don't feel ashamed if you tried these things. If Uncle Sam was dumb enough to invest trillions in their stimulus debacle—and dumb enough to keep appearing on TV to propose more failed programs—that should give you some solace. At least you are not the only one stranded in the past...

But you don't need to stay there. You can take action now to rectify the problem. You can study the techniques presented in this book. You can prepare for the future *now*. It is not too late...It is never too late.

2

ALIGNING WITH YOUR VISION

We hope you studied Chapter 1 closely because it lays the foundation for this chapter. To give you a quick review, let us say that the marketplace we are all operating in is no longer a local, state or national one. It is now a *global marketplace* and if you refuse to accept that fact—and adjust to it—your business will suffer accordingly.

Although the title of this book refers to stabilizing your business against a recession, what we are actually talking about is a global recession and you need to take action to not only prepare for a recession, but also to modify your company to make it more stable in this new environment we are entering. Even when there is no longer a recession raging, you will need a different business model to survive. In fact, we believe that some of the blame for the current recession should be placed on the global changes that have occurred since the advent of online communications.

These communication changes we have seen in the past decade have transformed how we all do business. Those businesses ignoring these changes are now in the process of going out of business. If their business models were too rigid to adjust (think of the US Postal Service), they are now failing or have already failed (think of Borders Bookstores).

Luckily, for most businesses it is not too late and changes can be made to accommodate the transformation that is occurring. If you make the changes outlined in this book, you can not only weather the next recession, but you can also transform your business to be in sync with the changes taking place—and you may even get ahead of your competitors!

We believe many people will acknowledge that there has been a tremendous change in the playing field we compete in, and we, as business owners, can no longer expect our local or regional communities to sustain our business. The Post Office is going out of business for a reason: *they are outdated because they refused to change.* The Internet has ushered in a new way to communicate, and the USPS failed to embrace that and take the lead. Now they are obsolete.

In the same fashion, these forces that led to the downfall of the Postal Service are pressuring every business in America. For this reason, you must make changes to your business, and the best way to do that is modify your business plan. How many business owners do you think have taken the time to form a strategy to modify their business to account for the recent changes we are discussing? Although many savvy business owners may already be discussing these changes, it is possible they have been too busy to design a formal plan to change their business. In fact, if you study some typical business plans, you will likely find that many businesses have not yet taken into account these global forces in a explicit and significant way by addressing them in their business plan.

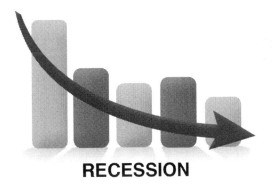

RECESSION

Several forces are at work against the small to medium sized business owner. The sad fact is that with the rising global debt burden, now spiraling out of control, the government has been hard-pressed to find additional revenue streams (outside of borrowing from China), and this has led to more pressure on taxpayers.

Government bureaucracies usually fail to downsize during times of economic trouble, at least not as much as the private sector does, and in their search for revenues to sustain their bloated organizations, they become more aggressive towards the private sector. When business owners feel like they are being targeted, they run for cover and start to expend more resources on tax *avoidance*.

This is a vicious circle that makes matters worse—all the more reason to stabilize your own company.

This additional pressure on private companies makes it even more difficult to find the time and resources to make drastic business model changes to accommodate the global transformation. Once you firmly believe that dramatic changes are underway, the only thing stopping you from transforming your business should be that you are under so much pressure, you don't have time. But we encourage you to make that time. We entreat you to do so, or you risk losing your entire business.

Here are the types of things you need to consider:

1. You must find a way to globalize your business model.
2. You must find a way to stabilize your revenue sources.

Globalizing Your Business Model

In order to discuss the topics relevant to globalization, we need to jump forward a little bit and tell you about some topics to come in a future chapter called Marketing in a Global Marketplace. In that chapter, we discuss cutting-edge marketing techniques that you can use to sell your products in the global market. But first you need to have products that will sell in that marketplace.

The changes you need to make will depend on your current business model and the products you sell. For example, if you currently offer electronic products, but your market is generally local, then it will be easier to globalize.

To illustrate the principles related to globalization, let

us consider a specific example—a fictitious business that you own and operate, call it AAA Graphics, and assume that you sell graphic design products such as logos, advertising layouts, and so forth.

We are going to make AAA Graphics an extreme case of non-globalization so that the changes needed in the company will be glaring. In reality, it is unlikely that owners of such a business will be as naive as we are going to make the leaders of AAA Graphics. However, We have been consultants in business for many years, and encountering such a business is possible, especially since it is a *family* business.

Suppose that you work for AAA Graphics and it currently advertises in the local newspaper and already has a large clientele established since it is a family business. Your father, who now works only as a consultant, founded the business and is passing it on to you. You attended graphics design school and you have recently returned home—fresh with your degree and full of trendy theories about graphic design—to take over as the primary leader of the company.

You did take some business management classes in college, so you understand the importance of having a solid business plan in place—something your father never thought he needed. Your father knows the local banker personally and was never required to submit a business plan when he went in to get financing for the business. It was a "good old boy" sort of transaction and most of it was done with a handshake and contracts no one ever bothered to read.

Unfortunately, your father's banker friend is along in

years and his health is faltering. Something else has been happening that you recognize as an ominous sign of the future: new business has been dwindling and even some of your established customers have not been calling, not as much as they used to. Since your father never really generated any reports that accurately measured the business, this trend is hard to see. The overall revenues have been dropping and your father knows something is wrong, but he does not know what.

You, on the other hand, feel that you are losing business to graphic designers in third-world countries because there are several online services that match up these contractors with American businesses and you heard in a local bar that one of your longtime clients hired one of these firms, and although unhappy with the result, was still putting out bids and not contacting local firms any longer.

Your main problem is that AAA Graphics relies too much on local revenue. Another critical problem is that your business model is becoming obsolete. Fortunately, you sell a product that will be easy to market and distribute online, and therefore easy to globalize.

Let us consider a particular product of AAA Graphics in order to illustrate the transformation in thinking you will need to undergo to transform your business. To illustrate globalization of a product, let us suggest one item: *Commissions on graphic designs sold*. With the advent of the Internet, many new businesses have emerged that sell graphics online at a low cost. Design companies all over the world can log onto these sites and purchase graphics for a particular project. They can perform a search and find hundreds of photos, illustrations, or videos that match the criteria of their current design project, and then select and buy what they need for a low cost, one that is much more affordable than what they pay to a local designer.

Since AAA Graphics has been in business for quite a while, they have ownership of many graphic designs they used in the initial stages of their design processes. Some of these online sites will make these designs available and will sell copies of these designs and send you a commission.

Making the designs you already own available on these sites would likely produce an instant new revenue source, one derived from anyone in the world with an Internet connection. In making these products available in this way, you have taken the first steps at globalizing your business.

Stabilizing Your Revenue Sources

Although you are now on the right track to globalize AAA Graphics, you still need to tackle another problem—*revenue stability*. We will get into the details of revenue stability in the next chapter, but here we need to discuss your vision so you can think differently about the future.

Let us give you a preview of revenue stability so you understand the concept and what is required with respect to your business plan and the vision you will need for AAA Graphics.

Revenue stability relates to the concept of a stable source of income. If you consider the current income stream of AAA Graphics, most of the stability is related to the fact that many of the client orders constitute repeat business, and these companies have been ordering advertising layouts and brochure designs from your father for years. But now many of these same clients have been pressured to reduce costs so they have gone online to find a cheaper supply of those products you have always delivered to them.

In short, your revenue streams were never very stable in the first place and the Internet has certainly caused further deterioration in those streams. Clients are no longer printing brochures to mail out; instead, they are running online promotions and doing most of it via electronic mail.

The fact is that even if the Internet—and the tremendous transformation it has ushered in—had never appeared on the landscape, your father could still have benefited from revenue stability principles. The reason is that AAA Graphics has no stable revenue sources. All the revenue comes from *local* clients that order a logo or an advertisement layout or a layout for the new printed catalog. The catalog orders were likely one of the most stable revenue sources since they usually came out periodically, but printed catalogs are becoming less common, so local web designers have taken some of the market.

In any case, to illustrate revenue stability, let us suggest several much more stable revenue sources. Currently orders can either come in at a high rate, or not a single order may come in for weeks. It all depends on who needs what. One way to stabilize revenue is to approach current clients and offer them package deals or subscriptions. For a fixed price, they can get a fixed number of ad layouts. This fixed price is paid on a periodic basis so they can be considered *subscriptions*.

This subscription money is a fixed revenue source because this revenue is committed for a certain period. If you put yourself in the position of a banker considering your application for a loan to expand your business, do you think he would appreciate the fact that you have contracts for $2,000 in subscription revenue each month for the next 18 months when your payment on the loan will be only several hundred a month? It will certainly make your payments easier.

These types of revenue streams make your financial position stronger and therefore you should structure your business in such a way to increase their prevalence.

Updating Your Business Plan

Once you have a firm understanding for the changes required for AAA Graphics, you will need to incorporate this thinking into your company business plan because you are going to need one. For example, although local banks are still in existence, and you will possibly get preference from them since you are local, in reality, you should try other sources—regional or national at least—for financing.

Think about it: in the same fashion as some of your clients are now searching for graphic products globally, you can also search for financing products in the same way (and legal services, and accounting services, and many other professional services as well; even assistance with the construction of the business plan itself). In fact, if you do not start to think *globally* on the expense side of the income statement, your bottom line will be significantly impacted there as well.

If you are going to obtain financing from a non-local source, you can expect that you will need a business plan, and in that plan you will need to incorporate the type of thinking discussed in this chapter. It will also be important that you finish reading this entire book before you construct our business plan, especially the chapter on Internet marketing. This knowledge will give you the appropriate foundational understanding to prepare a high quality business plan.

3

SALES AND REVENUE STABILITY

Revenue Stability

In this chapter, we will discuss methods to stabilize your revenue streams using the principles of revenue stability.

The Fundamental Principles of Revenue Stability

To understand the concept of revenue stability, first ask yourself the following question:

What is the primary source of revenue for your company?

You can get the answer to this question by first reviewing your invoice register. The various line items will encompass the various products and services your company generates revenue with.

If you own the company, you do not have to look at the register because you probably know in your mind.

If you sell a product or a service, the amount of predictability in your revenue streams depends in part on how you package them. If you advertise in the newspaper and wait for orders to come in over the phone or online, your revenue stream is probably not very predictable. You simply cannot determine what your sales will be in the future. You can estimate sales, but you cannot count on them. If the economy tanks, your sales may go down. Other forces may also affect sales.

However, if you also sell annual maintenance agreements for the products you sell, and you have 1,000 service agreements in place with clients in an assortment of business sectors, AND if those agreements specify that you will only service products that were purchased from your company, THEN your revenue stream is much more predictable. In order to get the service agreements, these customers must buy your products.

By selling service agreements, you have added value to your products and you have guaranteed a revenue stream from your services. You do not just sell a product and forget about it; instead, you sell a product and attach a service agreement to it, which represents future work—and future revenue. No matter what your product is, you can increase the stability of your revenue stream by adding value to it in this fashion.

Suppose you sell sandwiches from a food truck. You wait in your locations for customers to arrive. How can you add value to your food truck business to increase the predictability of your revenue stream?

You could give all your customers a discount card. Each time they purchase a sandwich, you punch a hole in their card, and when they get 10 punches, they receive a free sandwich. You have added value to your food truck products: In essence, each sandwich now includes 1/10 of a future sandwich.

Admittedly, you have not added much revenue stability, but it is some. You might consider expanding your operation so that you can offer more menu items. You could also set up contracts to park your trucks at various locations at fixed times. Some companies may need your services on-site for one reason or another. You could also consider working periodic events. You can possibly develop arrangements with local companies or other organizations to provide discounts in return for exclusive access to their employees.

Suppose you are a plumbing and heating specialist who waits for new business to come in over the phone. Suppose you offer all types of plumbing and heating services. How can you add value to increase the predictability of your revenue stream?

If you wait for potential clients to call and ask if you do this or that, then your revenue stream is totally unpredictable. If, however, you offer a service agreement, you will add predictability to your revenue streams. For example, suppose for a fixed amount of money, you will stop by a customer's location and service their furnace or other appliances. You do a tune-up and check for potential problems. Since most furnace manufactures recommend that the unit be serviced periodically—yet they do not offer to do it themselves—there is an opportunity. In the agreement, you offer to provide one free emergency visit per year.

Of course many people will buy a service contract because it is a great deal. And yes, that does transform your revenue stream into a fixed revenue stream. And this is the correct approach! If you can sell enough service agreements, you will convert your revenue stream from a highly unpredictable one to a highly predictable one.

Suppose that after a few years of selling these service agreements, you have 255 annual contracts in place, and the average revenue per contract is $175.

This translates to $44,625 dollars in gross revenue per year. Since you have done this for several years, you have found that the cost to service each contract is on average $75 per household. This means that your business is turning a profit of $100 per contract, or a total of $25,500 per year. All you have to do is take calls and dispatch your service technicians to the locations. You can still take calls from those without annual service agreements, and that revenue will be *in addition to* the fixed revenue from the service contracts.

Suppose you also sell plumbing and heating products. This is yet another revenue stream, so you have three revenue streams: (1) the annual service agreements, (2) the sporadic phone calls that come in for unscheduled service, and (3) your product sales.

In order to stabilize your revenue flows, think of it this way. What can you do to increase the value of your business? In other words, what would make your business more attractive to potential buyers?

To answer this question, put yourself in the place of a potential buyer. Would you rather buy a plumbing and heating company that gets all of its business over the phone, sporadically, or one with a ready-made stream of income and a list of predetermined (by the service agreements) jobs?

Obviously, you would opt for the business with guaranteed future work (assuming that you make a profit on the service calls). The reason is revenue stability. You don't have to worry about a stretch of bad business—when your phone doesn't ring—causing you to go broke.

To illustrate further, consider the insurance business. Insurance companies make huge profits, and their businesses are stable because of the *predictability* inherent in their revenue streams. Insurance policies are like service agreements, and in a way, you are simply selling insurance in the plumbing and heating business. You are "insuring" your products by backing them with your service.

But if you are purchasing a business, you want to have some amount of predictability in the revenue stream. This makes the business more stable and more valuable. If you already own a business, it also makes sense to build in as much predictability as possible. The reason for this is simple: you make more money in *both* good times and bad. Traditionally, contracts can be viewed as *assets* of a business, thus they increase the value.

It might help to consider the extreme cases, so let us do that here. After reading this section, what type of business do you believe has the most revenue stability?

The government is very stable, but let's take another, more realistic example: utility companies. Most *utility companies* have a monopoly and some type of agreement with the local or regional government where they operate a franchise in return for being subject to oversight of some sort.

Utility companies enjoy a high degree of revenue stability, and this is related to their monopolistic business model, so utility companies would be on the stable end of the revenue stability spectrum. What types of companies would be on the unstable end? Well, we have already discussed the food truck business. Other businesses with general revenue instability would be most non-franchised retail operations. They make their sales when a customer shows up at the door, but nothing guarantees that anyone will ever show up.

Hopefully, reading this section has increased your awareness of revenue stability and the importance it plays in the durability and marketability of your company. If you have survived the current recession (many are calling it a depression now), it is likely that your revenue streams already have some stability.

With this new understanding of revenue stability, you can take the appropriate actions to increase the revenue-stability of your products and services. But let us take this concept one step further. We do so in the next section.

Revenue Stability in a Global Marketplace

The basic principles of revenue stability also apply when addressing the topic of increasing stability in a *global* marketplace. The only difference is that you must accommodate global clients instead of local or regional ones. Globalizing your business is in itself a way to stabilize your revenues. Before we get into this topic, let us first discuss the relationship between products and services.

Products and Services

Any business can be categorized somewhere along the following spectrum:

Almost every business falls somewhere on this continuum. They offer some services with their products (even if they subcontract those services out), or they offer some products when they provide services. In reality, all businesses are selling products because services can be considered a product, although they are not physical.

A *product-oriented business* can be a manufacturer that takes raw materials and puts them together to create a new product, which they sell to distributors, who then sell the product to end customers or to other distributors. The manufacturer uses a fixed process to manufacture or distribute products. This process is independent of any one skill and it can be easily replicated when it is known.

A *service-oriented business* provides a service rather than a tangible, physical product. A physician, a plumber, or a hair stylist could be considered vendors of service-oriented products. But notice that most barbers and hair stylists have products for sale in their place of business. Admittedly, if you consider almost any type of business, you will see that most of them offer some combination of products and services.

So to answer the question about how your business generates its revenue, you have to first identify your products and or services. You should then develop a revenue stability plan.

Your first step might be to review your invoice register. All items that appear in the past year or so should be classified as products or services. Once a list of unique products and services is identified, you can go down the list and see if any other products or services can be developed that will add stability to the revenue stream.

For example, consider the plumbing and heating company we discussed in the previous section. This might be a list of product groups and services:

1. Annual service contracts
2. Plumbing fixtures
3. Furnace fixtures
4. On-call services to fix problems

We have already discussed the annual service contracts and how they took the business out of being primarily in "reaction mode," meaning that the customer now pays for a service agreement and then only calls when a problem arises. If no problems arise, then only one service call is necessary and no others are made. Thus more profit is generated.

Another product with a high level of revenue stability could be maintenance agreements on individual parts and fixtures. If a fixture or part is replaced on a service call, the service representative can offer to include a multi-year agreement to replace it.

Everyone has purchased an item, such as a television or other electronic product or appliance at Walmart and had the counter person at the checkout stand offer to sell them a multi-year service agreement that includes no-cost replacement.

These are revenue-stable service items, although there is the issue of non-repeatability (or the difficulty of selling additional service agreements on the same product after it expires). The revenue stability arises from the fact that a certain percentage of these products will be sold as add-ons. The plumbing & heating company can do the same.

In summary, here are the 3 steps you need to take to make your company more revenue-stable:

Step 1: identify your current products and services (*point A – where you are now*).

Step 2: identify additional products and services with a high level of revenue stability. Use the concept of salability as a gauge for how much revenue stability a proposed new product or service has (*point B – where you need to go*).

Step 3: identify a revenue-stability plan to include these products in your product line (*how you will get from point A to point B*). This plan will include advertising marketing campaigns, along with a time-line. Each product should be assessed and gauged for the amount of revenue stability it will bring. The list should be prioritized and those items with the highest stability should have top priority for implementation.

That discussion lays the foundation for the main topic of this section: *global revenue stability*. Many business owners are focused entirely on local or regional revenue streams. They do not consider global revenue streams—but they should. The problem with focusing only on local and regional revenue streams is that this approach leaves the business more vulnerable to regional economic swings. While many economic downturns are limited to the particular country or region of the world, far less are worldwide. It seems that some countries are always doing well, no matter how bad things get.

For this reason, it makes sense to *globalize* your revenue streams. This is more possible than ever now because of worldwide technology changes that many people have failed to recognize. The Internet and associated technologies have ushered in many opportunities. For example, most people might be thinking:

"How in the heck could a person ever globalize the revenue stream for a plumbing and heating business?"

Here is one way to do it: use technology to offer a product that has a high level of revenue stability. One product would be training services. To illustrate, We will use the example of Lynda.com. Lynda.com offers a very high quality line of training videos and almost all of their products are delivered over the Internet. A customer can buy individual classes, and have those classes shipped and delivered on a physical DVD, or they can also subscribe on a monthly or annual basis and have these training videos delivered electronically over an Internet connection. With a subscription, customers get full access to the entire training library, and Lynda.com offers new classes each month.

Along the same lines, a plumbing and heating company could develop a line of training videos, sell them over the Internet, and offer a subscription package as well. The topics for the videos are endless: fixing a leaky faucet, servicing a furnace, changing a fixture, installing a sink, etc. To make the subscription service more relevant and valuable, the topics could include new technology items. Here is another way to globalize, and it is very simple: get a website and sell products from that website. Most plumbing and heating companies would never expect to compete this way on a global scale, but if they would take the time to study the Internet marketing topics outlined later in this book, they might be surprised to learn they could sell a large amount of products using those techniques.

In particular, consider the concept of *Attraction Marketing*, which is a mainstream Internet marketing principle discussed later in this book. Here is a small preview of Attraction Marketing. Attraction Marketing is founded on the principle of providing a lot of free information in such a way that people come to view you as an expert in your niche area. When they experience a problem or need a solution in that niche area, they come to you for help: they buy your products.

Suppose you offer a plumbing and heating website with a popular forum and a large library of helpful, how-to plumbing and heating videos, and your forum membership grows to enjoy a large following. Many people around the world post questions on the forum and experts answer these questions. You are setting up a foundation for leveraging the principles of Attraction Marketing. Your blog, forum, or articles can reference your website and you can sell products there. More on this topic later…

MARKETING IN A GLOBAL MARKETPLACE

One way to stabilize your business is to expand your market *outside* of its current boundaries. Once you do this, you will need to take advantage of several emerging marketing tools.

The Evolving Global Business Framework

Never before in the history of mankind has it been so easy to expand into a global market. The Internet, social networks, and worldwide connectivity have enabled almost any business to expand its market. Yet the shocking truth is that not very many business leaders have taken the steps to do so.

We feel that if a business owner does not embrace these new technologies, they will ultimately fail. This is primarily because the younger generations are more highly connected—via cell phones, video games, social networking platforms, and other technical venues—and as they grow older, they will demand that those companies they buy from are also highly connected.

The Internet and Your Business

Earlier we discussed the demise of the Yellow Pages. Yes, there are new companies that have emerged to "replace"that function, like Yellowpages.com for example. However, these replacements do not actually replace the prior function entirely since the business world has been transformed in a fundamental way—a way that makes it impossible for these companies to reproduce the former Yellow Pages service.

These "replacement" companies may still possess contact information for businesses, but this contact information is no longer as complete as it once was (or nearly was). In the old days, prior to the Internet, you could open a phone book to the Yellow Pages in the back, and you would find a nearly complete list of businesses for the category and location in which you searched. In some towns, you may be able to get a pretty good list in the Yellow Pages, but the reality is this:

Google is replacing the function of the Yellow Pages.

And once every single business is listed on Google, they will have completely replaced the Yellow Pages. If you doubt this, consider the following story. We have a friend with a local plumbing business. The other day, he told us that Google has been hounding him to set up his free website on their servers. He then showed us the call log on his cell phone. Several times a week for that past month, they called him. Obviously Google is not just interested in getting his company name and phone number in their directory; they also want him to *move his website information* onto their servers.

Why?

Because they are savvy about the future and they know winning in business—in this rapidly evolving landscape—is no longer just about listing addresses and phone numbers. Google understands that eventually, every single business will have a website, and much of what they do—how they operate and who they transact business with—will take place (be "recorded") on that website.

If Google owns the servers, then they can place advertising on those "free" websites. Those websites will function like electronic real estate and Google wants to be the landlord. For these reasons, don't be surprised if Google makes a purchase of the top Web Host providers in the near future.

We are telling you this because Google is the leader and their actions are a good indication of the future, and a good indication of how the business playing field is evolving, and you will need to play the same game as everyone else is if you intend to stabilize your business and remain viable as a company in the future.

As of this writing, Google has not replaced the Yellow Pages function entirely, but their search facility is now the closest thing to it, and it is amazing how few business leaders have explicitly acknowledged this and are taking actions to proactively transform their business accordingly.

If you watch almost any teenager when it comes time to find a business address, they do not drive around looking for a phone booth with a tattered phone book dangling in the wind; rather, they Goggle the business name on their cell phone or use some other cell phone application. Often it is a GPS application that will also guide them to the business with accurate directions— they may even provide satellite and street-view photos in some cases (all provided by Google by the way).

Some of the more savvy adults from older generations do this also, but not with as high a frequency as the younger generations. This is the new world, the new business landscape as it is evolving, but so many business owners have failed to acknowledge it.

The Importance of Google Ranking

The bottom line is that you now need to appear in the top few pages of the Google search results when the searcher types in the keywords for your niche. You must do this to stabilize your business and prepare for the future.

Keywords are those words that identify the products you are selling or the services you are providing. For example, if someone has a flooding basement and they go to the Google search screen and type in "plumbing," they will get hundreds of millions of results, yet nothing to help them find a plumber in their own city.

If they type in "plumbers" they still will not get a list of local plumbers. They may see a link that says "Find Local Plumbers" and maybe they will click on that. But it is likely that this is a service that charges plumbers to be listed, thus they will not give the homeowner a complete list and will only provide contact information for those plumbers that have subscribed.

If the homeowner lives in Seattle and they type in "Seattle plumbers" they will likely get a list that is more relevant. Some actual plumbers will appear on page one of the results. There will also be those companies that charge plumbers to be in their list, and a lot of these are dead ends. Those savvy plumbers who have taken the time to do the right things (as outlined in this book) to get on page one of these search results are likely getting a lot more calls these days because the simple fact is that Google has replaced much of what the Yellow Pages did and Google is becoming more important in this respect as each day passes (i.e. consider our plumber friend and all the calls from Google?)

To get phone calls in the new world of business, and in particular, from the younger generations, you need to get a high ranking in the Google search results.

Internet Marketing Methods

So how do you get to the top of the Google search results?

It comes back to *keywords*. From the example above, you can see that certain keywords will bring different results. For every product and service, there are top keywords and you need to identify those keywords and then create Internet content with these keywords and the backlinks to your website. Backlinks are simply hyperlinks to your website, or live text that when clicked causes your site to be displayed on the screen. The entire logic of Google is founded on these backlinks and their "relevancy." A book could be written on the Google search and ranking algorithms alone, but basically, the more backlinks to your site—and the higher the quality of those links, or the more their relevancy—the higher your resulting rankings.

So you need to increase your backlinks. How do you do it?

Articles, Books, Marketing Lists, Etc.

To increase your backlinks, you create content that contains your keywords and the associated backlinks to your money site. This content is usually packaged in the form of articles, books, blog entries, blog comments, videos, and other forms. For example, you can write an article on how to replace a leaky faucet. Inside the article you have your physical address in Seattle and a hyperlink (backlink) to your website, where people can also obtain your contact information.

You could also find a forum on plumbing and post your article as a new posting there. You can comment on other posts and in each comment include a backlink to your website. When Google indexes the entire Internet (about once or twice a month these days) to build their search rankings, they will find these articles and your search ranking will increase for these keywords, and you will rise higher in the search results.

You can hire writers and Internet marketers to create and distribute this type of content, or you can take the time to do it yourself. Most people hire others simply because it is so time consuming. Several software tools are available for creating and distributing such content, and depending on your niche, you should consider using this software to increase your backlinks in this fashion.

The idea is to increase your backlinks, and there are several ways to do this. You can use (1) articles, (2) books, (3) periodic newsletters distributed to your marketing List (also known as an autoresponder campaign), (4) make blog postings or comments, or use other methods.

Article Marketing

Article marketing is one of the most common methods of increasing your backlinks. It is the process of writing articles with information around your niche and distributing these articles around various locations on the Internet. If you specialize in *business growth*, and you offer products and services to help businesses grow, then you would first determine your best keywords. You can do this by simply typing some key phrases into the Google search screen and then checking the results. When you get a list of your competitors, those are good keywords. But this is a hit-and-miss method.

An easier, more productive method would involve using automation tools to assist in your research. You can buy software or better yet, check out these popular keyword tracking sites: Wordtracker, Good Keywords, and Google's Keyword Tool. These sites keep track of what people are actually searching for and you can gather statistics for various keywords and keyword combinations. Once you have the right keywords, you can begin developing your article content. Again, you can write articles yourself or hire others; whatever you decide, the resulting articles should be populated with the best keywords.

You can also purchase software that will "spin" articles for you. Spinning is the process of generating multiple articles from a single article. You input the base article and the spinner software changes the words and paragraphs around to create multiple "new" articles. If your target market is not highly astute, you can use these sorts of automation tools, but if the readers in your niche are highly educated, you may want to hire professional writers to generate quality content for the articles. It will cost more, but the quality will be high and articles generated by spin software are often lower quality and this could reflect badly on you and hurt your business in the long run.

You can also get software that will automate the process of distributing your articles around to strategic locations. Instead of spending 15 minutes to upload your article to two or three article repositories, you can automatically upload to hundreds. Again, depending on your niche, you may be degrading the quality of your backlinks since recent Google updates can identify this type of activity and actually penalize you for this. You will get higher ranking scores if your article exists in only one or two places and is not overly duplicated. Some of the top article directories will not post your article if they find duplicate content posted elsewhere.

Book Marketing

Book marketing is another effective way to increase backlinks and your niche credibility. It involves the process of writing and using books as a marketing vehicle.

Book marketing allows you to use content from the book to power your Internet marketing efforts. You can take a chapter and create an eBook download from it. You can allow your website visitors to download this eBook in exchange for their name and email address. The chapters and sections of the book can also be divided into articles and these can be used to generate and direct traffic to your main site. Read more about this in the section, *List Marketing*.

Book marketing is one aspect of Internet marketing that not many marketers have taken advantage of. In fact, even though developing a book is less expensive than a typical article marketing campaign, most marketers have not done it. Also, the Google search algorithms are very sophisticated when it comes to parsing article marketing content; in comparison, keyword-optimized book content will get you top rankings much faster.

As a business leader, you are also somewhat of a public figure. This is exemplified when business operations become public events. Consider for example the BP oil spill in the Gulf of Mexico. This shed light on decisions made by those in control of the company. In BP's case it was a *negative* exposure, but public exposure can also be *positive*. When you write a book about your niche, the exposure you garner is usually positive and can add to your brand and ultimately your bottom line.

Below are some additional benefits associated with becoming a published author. All of them are positive with respect to increasing and stabilizing your business revenue streams:

1. *Credibility* - As a published author, you will enjoy a much higher level of credibility in your industry or niche. The act of compiling your thoughts enough to compose a book will not only signal to others that you are an expert; it will also force you to learn the concepts at a deeper level. This process essentially makes you an expert in those areas of your niche in which you are only familiar.

2. *Residual Income* – After you finish your book and it is available for sale at online distribution sites like Barnesandnobel.com, Amazon.com, and other book outlets, the sales can happen automatically and in the background to your normal activities. This increases revenue stream stability.

You may also choose to sell an electronic version of your manuscript in addition to the print version. The major search engines will index this electronic version, increasing your backlinks, and it can also be sold and distributed via a fully automated process. The sales can happen 24 hours a day, 7 days a week, all year long, and this is more in line with the process of globalization and revenue stability.

A tremendous transformation is taking place in the publishing industry (electronic media are replacing print media), and the process of self-publication is now very cost-effective. It is also viable to produce a book *only* for electronic distribution and skip the print version. The Kindle book reader is gaining momentum as a viable book delivery and distribution mechanism. You can also sell your print books at speaking engagements and other events for added income.

3. *Improved Media Opportunities* - Book authors are generally more sought after as speakers by media and other public organizations. At these organizations, professional interviewers tend to prefer published authors for interviews since they can read the book prior to the interview engagement. This gives them a better understanding about your message, and your message is delivered in a professional and highly consistent manner. If your title makes the best-seller list, you will enjoy increased speaking fees; even if you do not make a best-seller status, you should be able to garner higher fees since you are a book author.

As a business owner, it is likely that you already enjoy some local or regional recognition. As a published author, your recognition can be more easily expanded to a national or global level. This globalization of your personal (and business) branding will result in increased revenue stability.

Is it difficult to get a book published?

No. It is a much easier process than it was in the past. Print-On-Demand (POD) publishing allows you to upload your formatted book and only sell copies as they are ordered. In the past, you would need to place a large order for books (usually more than 500) and then distribute them yourself or via your publisher. If you revised the book, all those unsold copies were no longer relevant and you needed to run a new batch.

Also, using POD methods, an author can bypass the traditional methods of getting published, and get their title listed on Amazon directly. In the old days, you needed to find a publisher and/or an agent first, and that process was difficult for many new writers.

Some people would argue that the traditional publishing route is a vetting process that enables only higher quality books to ultimately reach the market. The problem with the older method is that it can take years for a book to finally reach the market, if it ever makes it at all. If you publish directly, via POD methods, you may enjoy a lot of sales and this may prompt a traditional publishing deal or a contract with an agent.

List Marketing

List marketing is simply the electronic version of traditional mail marketing. There is this huge difference however: *the cost is much lower now.*

You can manage and communicate with a list of several thousand prospects for less than $100 per month. To do something comparable in the traditional print world would run in the thousands of dollars. In an earlier chapter, we discussed the demise of the United States Postal Service. List marketing, and other electronic forms of communication are primary reasons these bloated government bureaucracies are going bankrupt. They are essentially a government-protected monopoly and thus not highly motivated (if motivated at all) to innovate. This clear lack of innovation is also a reason for their demise.

In any case, there is now a tremendous opportunity for the average business to engage in high quality, low-cost List marketing and targeted communications with a large number of prospects. You can send weekly or daily (depending on your product) communications with valued content to prospects on your List. This content can include links to your money site. We will give you a successful example of List marketing: Costco.com. You can visit their site and sign up for their List. You will then receive weekly (more often actually) offers that include discounts and online-only offers. This is an example of a retailer who is engaged in a very effective List marketing campaign.

List marketing is also effective for other products and services. Business growth would be an example of a niche for this type of Internet marketing. List marketing is a key component in an emerging section of Internet marketing called "Attraction Marketing."

Attraction Marketing

Attraction Marketing is a powerful new category of Internet marketing. It refers to a little-known process that will ultimately result in increased sales for your products and services.

Wikepedia.com defines Attraction Marketing as follows:

"Attraction Marketing is the use of marketing techniques specifically designed to teach the customer what you are doing and how a service or product will benefit them well before they purchase it."

Note the key word "before." This system relies on you setting yourself up as an expert in your niche, gaining credibility with your prospects, and becoming the "go-to expert" for them when they need a solution.

The implementation of Attraction Marketing is based on several principles. Here are two of the most important:

1. Offer an abundance of quality content.
2. Offer multi-tiered products and/or services.

Offer an abundance of quality content.

As mentioned above, you would distribute your content all over the Internet and use software tools and outsourcing services to accomplish this. You would also have a website where you offer an abundance of valuable content for free. Your website may have a forum with many informative postings related to your product(s) and/or service(s).

The object here is to establish yourself as a go-to expert on the topics related to your niche. If you are a business growth expert, then when someone has a business growth problem, they visit your forum and post a description of their problem and wait for someone to tell them about the best solution. Possibly you offer how-to videos and other information on your site. Maybe an "Ask-the-Expert" section in the forum where you answer questions.

Offer multi-tiered products and/or services.

You have a simple lower-priced item (or items) that you sell at a high volume and low margin. Call this "Product A." The profits from Product A are used to fund your Attraction Marketing system—your website fees, contracted services, and other expenses. You also offer a higher-priced product (or products), and this is how you make your big money—the money you will retire on. Call this higher-priced item "Product B." If you are in the business development field, Product B might be consulting services.

You use all the available Internet marketing tools to promote and sell Product A, and you do not overtly promote Product B; instead, you are promoting it *covertly*.

This approach relies on the fact that people generally do not like to be overtly "sold" on larger products (or even small ones). Buyers like to feel they are in control of the buying process. If you push Product B too hard, your prospects will sense it and show resistance. If instead, you establish yourself as an expert in the field surrounding Product B, and you offer rich information on your site about Product B, grateful prospects will find it, and since you have established yourself as an expert, they will conclude on their own to buy Product B. Offering quality content, and establishing yourself as an expert forms the foundation of a successful Attraction Marketing system.

Your sales funnel would thus be constructed as follows: You would create a Landing Page, or a simple 1-page website, on which you collect names and email addresses. Visitors would opt-in to your email List in exchange for some piece of quality content. You would then direct these opt-in prospects to your sales page for Product A. These members would be added to your autoresponder List and sent high-value directed content as described above.

Over time, you would be perceived as more of an expert since this content would have backlinks to your website and other quality content. Eventually, they would find and buy Product B.

5

HUMAN RESOURCES

One of the most important components of any business is human resources. A good employee can have a tremendous *positive* impact on a business, and a bad employee can have a tremendous *negative* impact. For example, a top sales representative can make the difference between achieving an annual profit and suffering a net loss. Considering the topic of this book—i.e. methods to recession-proof your business—we will consider the various forces at work in the new business world of globalization and diversification with respect to human resources.

The Required Skill Sets

Note that several methodologies have been presented so far in earlier chapters. Most, if not all of these, are related to Internet marketing methods. We have discussed the fact that you will need to have your business located at the top of the search engine results for the keywords in your niche. Given the unique human resource requirements of achieving this goal, it is unlikely that you will be able to retain the skills necessary by hiring locally. Luckily, by retaining and contracting with individuals online, you can fulfill much of the human resources required to stabilize your business.

To achieve higher rankings in the search engine results, you will eventually need to retain personnel with the below skills. It is unlikely that you will find one individual with all of these skills; rather, you will need to develop relationships with *several* contractors.

1. A general understanding of Internet marketing concepts
2. Website layout and programming
   - PayPal or other payment processor integration
   - Hosting account management
   - Shopping cart setup and management
3. Graphic design
   - Logos
   - Website banners
   - Sales/Landing pages
   - Newsletters
   - Book covers
   - Letterhead
4. Professional copywriting skills
   - Website copy
   - Email campaigns
   - Newsletters

- Book/eBook content
- Press releases
5. List management

Posting to Online Job Sites

Individuals with the above skill set can be found by working through online job sites. Several job sites exist, and you can post your projects there and retain individuals with the above skills. The main problem you will encounter will be finding one individual who is well versed in all of these areas. As a result, your business efforts may end up disjoint, and this can result in higher expenses due to unnecessary rework. If you find competent individuals in these areas, you should do everything possible to develop a relationship and retain them for the long-term. Below are some tips for posting your projects on online job sites.

Do not low-ball. Note that many companies from third-world countries actively bid on these job sites, and they use US-based addresses, so it is difficult to verify that you are in fact hiring native-English speakers for your writing projects. Some foreign companies may be able to produce good copy, but the vast majority of them will produce substandard products that contain garbled verbs and adjectives, so it is really a "buyer beware" situation. These foreign companies will usually bid very low since their costs are lower in depressed economies. In any case, if you post your project with a maximum price that is low, the higher quality writers / designers will probably avoid your project altogether, and you will never get a bid from them. Since you want English-speaking contractors to at least consider your project, do not set a maximum price that is low; instead, post the project with no limit on price. Many people post projects with low maximum prices thinking they will hold down costs, when in fact they are not. What happens is they get substandard workers, and after several failures, and a loss of money, they realize they need to pay a more fair price. Why limit your project this way? Leave it open and see what bids come in.

Be clear about deliverables and time frame. Specify exactly what it is you are hiring for. If it is to write a book, let potential contractors know the length of the book, if you need publishing assistance, what your general time frame is, what format the product should be delivered in, and so forth. Quality contractors will use a formal Service Agreement to specify (1) the exact deliverables, (2) the time frame, and (3) the payment schedule. Once you have established an ongoing relationship with a quality contractor, you can loosen the formalities and just specify dates, times, and payments via email messages, but for the first few projects, you should use a formal Service

Agreement. This helps the communication process and avoids problems in the future. Highly skilled freelancers need these communication tools to produce quality products.

Break large projects into smaller ones. If you have a large project, break it down into components that are easier to manage. Avoid making a huge down payment and then discovering that your contractor is inadequate or lacks the required skills. Suppose you have a book to write and you need to hire a ghostwriter. If you hire one based upon their website and writer Bio, you may find that it is all misinformation (or grossly overstated). Possibly, the ghostwriter never even passed grammar school; possibly they are writing your book from prison. You might even make a large down payment and in return they ultimately give you gibberish for a book. This failure would be partly your fault. The best approach on large projects is to hire several candidates to produce a smaller portion of the project deliverables, and then hire the best of these candidates based on the result. If you have a large writing project, you might even consider hiring a professional editor to evaluate the candidates. Considering that the fees for ghostwriting a business book can run into the tens of thousands, this would be a very good investment. The same is true for website development, or other large Internet marketing campaigns.

Using Escrow. Escrow is a good idea, but in reality, no quality contractors will likely agree to perform work until you pay them some money up front. Many of the online job sites make a big deal about their transactions being safe since you get to use escrow, but it is hardly safe for the freelancer. The problem they have is that they could perform work for money sitting in escrow, but they may never get it. If a client dies or changes his mind, or goes bankrupt, or whatever, the contractor will be out the work they did. Freelancers in third-world countries will often perform work for money in escrow, but often the quality is very low. Until the money is in the bank account of the freelancer, it is at risk. Many quality freelances will not even bid on a project that specifies the use of escrow. When transacting business, the money is not "real" until it is in your bank account. This is not only true in the online world, but also in the real world. As a result, most quality freelancers will require some percentage of the project fees to be PAID before work begins.

Move future projects into a direct relationship. The online job sites are good for making connections, but their fees are high, and you will get far better prices if you can deal directly with the contractor(s). After you perform one or two projects through the online job sites, you should approach the next project directly. You can use payment processors like PayPal to send money directly to a contractor.

Post on multiple sites. You should post your project(s) on multiple online job sites and not just one. Some con-tractors use only one site, so if you post it everywhere, you will have your project exposed to the highest audience, These online job sites (currently) do not charge the client; rather, they deduct their fees from the contractor, so it is essentially free to post a job. You can pay extra to get priority postings, but it is not necessary.

Hire only native-English speakers. English is the

gold standard when it comes to most of the skills you need. Some are graphics-related, but most require quality writing skills. No matter how long a non-native English contractor has been writing in English, most of them will always garble their written words, and the result will reflect badly on your business. The fact is, most of the techniques outlined in this book require writing, and that writing should be top quality. Don't believe that you can only get economical pricing if you hire workers from a third-world country. Many American citizens are now competing effectively in these markets and have adjusted their prices accordingly. The other issue you will encounter when hiring non-English speakers is the project communication will also suffer. This means that you can hire from a third-world country to create a software program and your project will still suffer, even though it is mostly technical. Unfortunately, the various cultures have different expectations with amount of pay and this may ultimately create a problem. If you cannot effectively communicate with someone who is doing work for you, then the quality of that work will likely suffer, and there will likely be problems over payments.

Stabilizing Revenue Streams With Products

Let us now consider how various products can bring an increased amount of stability to a business. We are going to use a fictitious company and product, but this example is based on a real company and product from the US business world. The company used for this example is The Coffee Bean & Tea Leaf®, and the product is the *kaldi* single-serve beverage system. The below example is based on this product, but the details do not exactly follow what this company has done. We have extended the example to illustrate the concepts of this book.

The company sells hot coffee, tea, and cold blended drinks. The business began operating roughly 50 years ago as a single café, and now it offers drive-through and in-store service with a sit-down, café-like setting. All of the current stores are company-owned.

Various business changes will allow them to grow, diversify, and stabilize. We will consider the following two product categories.

1. Franchise Opportunities
2. Other Products

Both of these categories provide a tremendous amount of growth, diversification, and stabilization, and we can now consider the benefits and human resource requirements of each option.

Franchise Opportunities

Offering franchises will create another revenue stream above and beyond the revenues generated from the sale of their current product line. Currently, all revenues are generated from the company-owned stores selling various drinks.

Franchising will allow the company to expand into various multi-national locations. In essence, by franchising, they are turning their core business and brand into a product. We could address this in the next section as a separate product, but we will do so here as the concepts and human resource issues are much different.

With respect to making the business more recession-proof, franchising is an excellent method. By selling franchises, the cost of delivering products and managing the businesses—and the associated human resources—is transferred from the core business to the franchisee. Essentially, the owners of the core business can sell their business template and while having very little investment, retain a portion of the profits derived at the franchise.

The human resource requirements would be to support the franchises in various areas, including the following:

(1) Training – The franchise owners will require some amount of training in how to operate the business. The employees of the franchise will also require training in the various employee roles and positions. Existing training facilities and resources for the core business can be scaled to accommodate franchise requirements.

(2) Product Supply – The franchises will need to be adequately supplied with company products. Usually, the current product supply chain can be modified and extended to accommodate franchise operations.

(3) Branding Support – This includes advertising campaigns and branding material. The local franchises will benefit from national advertising campaigns, but will supplement those activities with local marketing and advertising.

(4) Product Support – When certain problems arise at a franchise with products, the main company will need to support those products and resolve those problems. Usually, the current support system can be extended to facilitate franchise operation support and problem reso-

lution.

Other Products

Here are the related products that can be developed and sold by Coffee Bean & Tea Leaf®:

- Coffee machines
- Coffee and other drinks

First of all, the business can create a coffee machine product that duplicates the core products sold in the company stores (and in the franchise locations). They can also create other products related to this core product.

These additional products will create new revenue streams that will further stabilize the business and protect it from local, regional, and national fluctuations in the economy (like a recession). These products will also open the door to a tremendous opportunity to implement some of the other strategies discussed in this book.

For example, an excellent way to increase revenue stability is to create a subscription-based revenue source. Suppose that the core business sells a total of 40 different drinks, and they develop a machine that will deliver each of these drinks. The owner of such a machine only needs to buy a capsule, insert the capsule into the machine, add water, push a button, and the machine delivers the drink.

These machines—and the associated capsules— can be sold in the company-owned stores, and in the franchise stores. They can also be sold online. The buyer of a machine can return to the store to purchase capsules, or they can purchase a monthly subscription, managed online, and have the capsules delivered to their doorstep.

The business has now created a subscription-based product and this will ultimately increase the value of the company dramatically.

Why?

Because when a business is ultimately sold, the buyer will evaluate how much the company is worth. When a business is valued for acquisition, subscriptions are considered as fixed revenue streams and are highly sought after by potential buyers.

The reason is simple and can be illustrated with an example. Suppose you want to purchase a business and you are considering two potential candidates. The first candidate is a doctor's office. The doctor's office has three prominent doctors. All have agreed to continue working in the business after you purchase it, but only for a limited amount of time. During that time, you will need to introduce new doctors and try to transition the patients from the old doctors to the new doctors.

Since the revenue stream of a doctor's office is highly dependent on the doctors themselves, the acquired revenues will be vulnerable. Suppose you purchase this doctor's office and a week later, a tornado destroys the office and incapacitates all three physicians. You will have nothing left of the business you just purchased. You will likely lose most of the patients since they are often loyal to a particular physician and not the office itself. In contrast, consider the coffee business described above.

Where is the customer loyalty?

It is in the brand. It is in the subscription. If a tornado wipes out one of the stores, there are many others, all with individual revenue streams. After you rebuild the destroyed store with insurance money, it is likely that most of the former customers will return and the revenue stream will be reestablished. The revenue stream from the subscribers will hardly be affected at all, unless of course the main supply warehouse is destroyed, but now we are considering disaster recovery scenarios, and the fact remains that the coffee business is inherently more stable than a doctor's office.

The beauty of introducing a subscriber-based revenue stream is that these subscription revenues are fixed, and they can originate from anywhere in the world.

Social Networking

The introduction of subscriber-based revenue streams also opens the door to tremendous opportunities for social networking. If the monthly subscription is designed such that each subscriber selects a monthly allotment of capsules, which are then delivered to their home, then an online form of communication is a co-requisite to owning a machine and a subscription.

Each month, the subscriber logs onto his or her account to specify that month's order. This presents a very high quality opportunity for further marketing efforts. You now have these customers' attention, and you can use this to sell more products. If they use their email addresses as their login, then you can also send marketing materials to them on a periodic basis, possibly a newsletter or an autoresponder campaign. As mentioned previously, Costco. com is an excellent example of a company with a very successful List management system.

By establishing this online communication vehicle,

you have created the foundation for using all of the techniques discussed earlier in this book (Attraction Marketing, List marketing, others). Thus, you have created the foundation for further stability and growth.

Each subscriber has effectively become a member of your company's "social network." You can then direct them to your company Facebook and Twitter sites and contact them with various marketing methods. All of the skills outlined above can be outsourced to contractors from online job sites, or these skills can be developed internally in the form of full-time (or part-time), permanent (or temporary) employees.

In addition to the core products of the coffee machine and capsules, other products can be marketed. Making drinks is not always a straightforward process, so there is also a need for training materials. These materials can be presented in an online forum where subscribers can post questions or procedures for making new drinks. Information and procedures can be exchanged between members of your online community. You have just created a high-quality Attraction Marketing system.

In essence, by using the techniques outlined in this book, the basic business model of a local drive-thru (and in-store) delivery of coffee and tea products can be transformed into a global, subscriber-based (and online-supported) business community in which customers interact and socialize. In making this transformation, the business increases its value, its stability, and thus its overall ability to survive in future adverse economic conditions.

6

Expense Reduction
Methods

Although many business leaders try to keep their business running at an optimal state, keeping expenses to the bare minimum, the reality is that almost any business will have waste when it comes to unnecessary expenses. There are several reasons for this.

First, over time processes evolve *internally*, and even if they were originally designed and implemented in an optimal form, it is likely that the process evolution has rendered the steps and required component expenses less than optimal.

Second, conditions also change *externally* (in the marketplace) to make processes less than optimal. For example, suppose you use an electronic component during a core business process. Over time, less expensive components will likely become available to meet the needs of that particular business process. If no one is proactively managing this, and replacing old parts with newer, more efficient ones, resources will likely be wasted.

While the above forms of waste are *procedural* in nature, the third form of waste is more *operational*. Operational waste occurs as a result of management decisions and other basic methods of doing business.

Procedural Expense Reduction

Every business contains operating procedures or processes, which are a series of steps taken to achieve a desired result. These procedures can be streamlined and optimized into formal "work standards." Formal work standards are documented, and implemented into daily business operations. Their primary function is to guide workers through each step of a business procedure. The benefits of these work standards are (1) they provide an optimal method of training people and (2) they effectively manage output in a consistent and repeatable fashion.

Once all of the business procedures are documented in formal work standards and implemented into the workflow, business processes will run faster and more efficiently with fewer mistakes and less waste.

The methods for standardizing processes and creating effective work procedures can be fairly complicated, and these details fall outside the scope of this book. We note them here to make you aware of them, but we recommend that you contact consultants with the required credentials to help you build work standards for your business. We are well trained in all the various methods of expense reduction discussed in this book, and if you need assistance with this process, please refer to our contact information included in this book.

Operational Expense Reduction

Beyond process optimization using work standards to streamline business procedures, various non-specific operational cost-cutting measures can be taken to reduce expenses. These are changes that can be implemented in most business environments to reduce expenses. This section will review some of these measures. Some may be applicable to your business while others may not be.

Telecommunications Overhaul

The telecommunications configurations (data, voice, other) of most medium-sized businesses over time tend to become disorganized. There is no inefficient process at work here, just the normal chaos that results from making ongoing modifications to accommodate growth or change in the existing network(s).

Although some businesses keep their telecommunications functions well organized, most are in disarray and a significant amount of savings can be realized quickly by performing an overhaul.

If your company has a telephone system with a lot of incoming lines, it is likely these lines are not configured optimally, and by implementing recent innovations in alternative forms of communication, some of the wasted resources associated with those lines can be recovered.

If you own or manage a service business, many of those telephone lines that come into the system are likely being used by the customer support and customer service departments, but staff members likely utilize other methods of communicating such as email and personal cell phones, among others.

The goal is to identify this unused capacity and disconnect those resources associated with it. With any revamp of technology configurations, there will possibly be many long-term improvements and a few highly productive (in terms of cost reduction) changes that can be made quickly and easily.

For example, possibly you have a phone system that is maintained and programmed by an external company. Suppose you bought it from a telecommunications vendor and they programmed it initially, and your local Information Systems department performs minor maintenance but nothing complicated; maybe they program telephone extensions and manage simple call groups or some other superficial function.

Although you may believe your local support people have been keeping everything optimized, this is hardly ever the case due to the complexity of telecommunications systems and the chaos associated with the large number of changes taking place in a typical business.

To achieve quick cost reductions, have the vendor of your phone system perform a quick resource evaluation to determine any possible optimizations.

This process can be messy because you will be working from two sides. On one side, you have the actual phone system and the physical lines and other resources; on the other, you have all the monthly bills from the telecommunications provider.

The other aspect is the actual business environment and what it requires in terms of resources. This is the part that can get complicated, but there may also be some savings there as well. Usually, matching the requirements of the business environment to the resources is a complicated process given business growth and other key factors.

Example – Optimization of a Telecommunications System

To illustrate this process, we will give you an example, and to keep it simple, we will tell you about only one aspect of the many things we evaluated. Our goal was to optimize the telecommunications system in a company and to reduce short and long-term costs. Although the actual overhaul investigated various aspects of the voice and data configuration, we will focus only on the voice configuration we encountered.

Our first step was to identify the physical phone lines the company was paying for. We gathered together the various monthly statements for these lines. Upon reviewing them, we discovered that the company was paying for approximately 70 incoming physical lines (voice/fax/other) in addition to their Internet data lines.

This particular telephone system was a bit older and had about 40 lines coming in, with several fax machines located throughout the two main office buildings, along with some other individual lines that were hooked to various telephone management programs, but the other lines listed on the statements were a mystery.

After a thorough investigation and search, we determined that the remaining lines were being paid for but not being used anywhere in the building! They had been installed years before the overhaul for various reasons but had somehow never been disconnected. They simply terminated at the wall, and were still carrying a signal, but no device was hooked to them. And they were still being paid for! The total savings on these lines alone translated to several hundred dollars per month, and thousands per year.

We also determined a better way to optimize resources on the entire phone system was to merge voice and data online, and we were able to eliminate more expenses right away by evenly balancing the overall system load. We ultimately installed a new system, but that came months later in the overall process. We use this example to illustrate the extreme savings that may be lying just under the surface and easy to find. You can also work with vendors to obtain volume discounts and term agreements for additional savings.

Another thing you can do for quick savings in the telecommunications area is to terminate any cell phone accounts that are being paid for by the company.

Even though most will be on a term agreement, you can still save by terminating them early and stopping all activity on these accounts. This will return transparency to the process and eliminate a huge expense. It will also put a stop to a lot of personal phone calls and texting, along with the time wasted.

Company Automobiles

Many companies provide vehicles to employees. These can be driven full time by the sales force or trucks driven home and parked at night by the installation crew.

If your company is under any kind of financial duress, or possibly undergoing a bankruptcy, this program needs to be terminated immediately. At this point in the game, your employees should already be aware that the company is in danger of failing entirely, so they should fully understand your actions.

If you need a talking point when notifying them that the vehicles will be cut, tell them this: Economic times are difficult, and if the company ultimately fails, these vehicles will likely end up going to the creditors. Instead of allowing that to happen, these vehicles can be sold now to generate needed cash. Isn't it better to liquidate them and pay the money out in salaries and other expenses that will perpetuate the business? It is unlikely that anyone will argue with this line of reasoning.

Terminate Lines of Credit

Start with credit cards and make sure to include any form of buying on credit. During times of financial hardship, no employee other than the owner should have the ability to purchase anything on credit.

Insurance Restructuring

Another area where quick cost reductions can be realized is in the area of insurance. As with telecommunications, you will find that in any medium-sized business, conditions evolve over time and there are likely some easy changes that can be made to free up quick cash in the form of cost reductions.

If you have one insurance agent who handles all of your insurance needs, contact that agent and tell him or her that you are restructuring your coverage and you would like to rewrite the policies. You want to see what everything will cost with different deductibles. Now get proposals from other insurance agencies and compare those to this proposal. You will likely find quick savings either with the higher deductibles or between underwriters, or with some combination of those.

(Re)Negotiate Supplier Contracts

If you resell and distribute enough products to warrant staffing a full-time purchasing department, and you have vendor contracts in place, then you can find some immediate savings here as well. Even if you are not quite large enough to have a purchasing department and you handle these agreements yourself, you can do this.

If you indicate to vendors that times are difficult and you are taking actions to remain in business, these vendors will likely be amenable to the idea of lowering your prices for their products because if you go out of business, they will lose a customer (the fact that you have purchasing agreements implies you are a large customer of theirs). This can be a powerful incentive.

All the adjustments in their pricing schedule will translate to lower costs for you, which ultimately appears in your bottom line as increased net profits.

Lease Agreements

As you have negotiated with your vendors, you can also negotiate with leaseholders to lower your lease agreements. Your landlords, or other leaseholders would likely rather lower your rates than lose you as a customer.

Whatever property you are leasing, they would likely rather keep the steady form of income than have to spend the time and resources to find another tenant.

Unnecessary Technology Upgrades

If you are near the end of the fiscal year, all of your managers will likely have plans to make purchases for tax or budgetary reasons. Put a stop to this. If your current technology is adequate to process the daily business transactions, then you likely do not need to upgrade for 18 months.

According to Moore's law, the speed of technology doubles every 18 months, and conversely the cost should decrease by one half. Even so, it is unlikely that processing needs exceed your current computing resources.

In reality, all computers reached a threshold in the last part of the 1990s. At that point the standard computer systems were powerful enough to run all the applications necessary to operate a business. What you see now is an endless rollout of new operating systems (Windows 95, Windows 97, Windows XP, Windows Vista, Windows 7—and this spans only about 10 years) and other gimmicks to confuse the public and generate revenues.

These new operating systems just get bigger and slower and it is the operating systems that require bigger and new computers. The business applications that run on the operating systems do not require any new upgrades. The computers of 1999 were fast enough to run it all. Your MS Word program would run almost as well on a computer of five years in the past as it will on one of five years in the future.

The bottom line in all of this: Do not upgrade your operating systems on your workstations; you can keep those computers for a very long time. This pattern is replicated on most other computer architectures besides the PC as well (midranges and mainframes), although not to the degree it occurs with the personal computer. In short, you can significantly reduce costs by putting a stop to the upgrade craziness.

Outsourcing

We have already addressed outsourcing to some degree in the Human Resources section. Basically, you need to perform an analysis of every function of your organization to determine if you can outsource each process via online job sites. WE say online because this is where you will realize the biggest benefits. There is also another side to this. Most firms retain an ongoing cast of consultants who help with various tasks or perform them entirely. These consultants should be eliminated because their hourly rate is typically very high and often their function is not essential. Remember, those functions you can outsource on the Internet will likely result in significant cost savings.

Travel

Since travel expenses are probably one of your highest expenses besides employee-related costs and product costs, you need to impose a moratorium on travel expenses immediately. Announce it to your staff and senior managers like this (short and simple): "Tele-commute"

Although transacting business in person will always surpass, in quality, virtual transactions and remote electronic communications, you can do this during a recession or other difficult economic times.

Implement the 80-20 Rule

If you provide services to your customers, then stop providing these services to any customers who do not pay on time. This is simply implementation of the 80-20 Rule:

20% of your customers provide 80% of your revenue

Your task is to identify those customers who fall in the 20% category. Conversely, 20% of your customers create 80% of your problems. Again, you need to identify those who fall in this lower 20% sector. These customers have to go immediately, and you should implement structural and procedural changes that will discourage this lower 20% sector from interacting with your business.

Remember, you can retain the right to refuse service to anyone, and you can exercise this right on these lower 20%. If you are new to the 80-20 Rule, think of it this way. Suppose you place all of your customers on a spectrum so they are ranked by their value to your business. You can rank them using various measures and criteria, so this would not be a straightforward process. But suppose you identify your top five customers; you should be able to do that.

What makes them your top five customers?

Do they purchase a lot of products?

Do they pay everything on time?

Do they pay in advance and operate under contract?

There are multiple things that make a good customer, but usually the one outstanding factor is that you make a lot of money from them.

Now, consider your *worst* five customers. We can already tell you that probably the top criteria that makes them a bad customer is they do not pay their bills or honor their agreements. To reduce expenses and operate in a leaner fashion, you simply have to deny services and products to those that fall on the lower end of the customer quality spectrum, and conversely, you need to focus resources on those customers who fall at the upper end.

The actual cutoff line will be different for each company, as will the particular criteria used to sort and rank your customer list. You do need to do this, however, and implementing this change will save you a significant amount of cash.

Hopefully, during this streamlining process, you will remove the lower 20% of your service offerings, the worst of your products and product lines, and probably much more. Customers who eat up your service and support resources while sitting persistently at the top of your accounts receivable register are just those customers that you must jettison during difficult times.

7

Debt Reduction Methods

Most business owners do not realize that all commercial debt is negotiable, and this is especially true when a company is undergoing times of duress. Our experience indicates that by following the right procedures, you can reduce your overall commercial debt burden by over 60%.

If you want a detailed treatment of this topic, you can order the book, *Commercial Debt Negotiation* by André Larabie (coauthor of this book). Mr. Larabie has implemented this process successfully for over 20 years. We will present here an abbreviated description of his proven commercial debt-reduction techniques.

Note that although all of a business's debt is considered to be "commercial," you, as business owner, may have guaranteed some portion of the overall debt, and this system will address this aspect of commercial debt.

Understanding Your Overall Debt Burden

To restructure your commercial debt burden, you must first have a complete understanding of your overall debt picture. To get this, construct a list of all the creditors.

This list should include the following information:

- *Every debt* – Include all the commercial debt you have, whether it is with leasing companies or asset-based lending companies.

- *All short-term and long-term debt* – This can come from your accounts payable records.

The main goal is to get everything down on paper so that we know:

- The amounts of the individual obligations
- To whom you owe these amounts
- Your total debt burden

Assigning Priorities

Next, we are going to prioritize all of the outstanding commercial debt for your company. For each payable account, note whether you incurred the debt in the last 30 days, 60 days, 90 days, or more.

You also have to determine which of these debts—if

you are able to negotiate them into a more favorable state—can help to save your business. These will become your priorities during the negotiation process, and it is important that you respect these priorities. After you have a list of each and every obligation, go through the list and assign a number 1 to those creditors that are the most important to your business, assign a priority number 2 to those with medium importance, and a priority 3 to the least important.

You will move the number 1 creditors to the top of the list. Then place the number 2 creditors below those, followed by the number 3s.

The Priority 1 Creditors

The priority number 1 accounts should be those that are of the utmost importance to your business, so critical to your operation that if you do not salvage the relationship, the fallout will likely cause the end of your business.

Since they are at the top of the list, you have to address them differently than if they were lower on the list. Those creditors on the lower section of the list are not a priority, so even if you don't pay them back, it is not going to kill your business.

So first you identify all those high priority creditors that can shut you down. You are not able to obtain their product or service anywhere else. After you have identified all of these number 1s, make another pass through the number 1s on the list and highlight the most critical of those. So you prioritize the 1s *within* the 1s.

The Priority 2 Creditors

The priority 2 creditors are those creditors that are critical to your operation such that if your relationship with them is severed, it will disrupt your operation, but the degraded relationship will not cause your company to shut down.

From a business standpoint, you do need them from time to time, so if you don't settle with them, you will likely be able to survive without doing business with them, at least on a short-term basis. These are the creditors that you likely don't use every month; rather, you need them about every three to six months to carry on business. Give these creditors a number 2 priority.

In other words, if you will eventually need to buy some critical material or service from them—but not right away—you can put them lower on the list than the number 1 creditors. For the priority 2 creditors, if you cut their product or service off, it will cause some disruption in your business. Maybe your operation won't run as smoothly, but it will not completely STOP you from operating.

The Priority 3 Creditors

The priority 3 creditors are the creditors that remain on the list after you have identified the priority 1 and the priority 2 creditors. These can be described as follows: If you never do business with a priority 3 creditor, it should not affect your ability to operate your business.

Other Debts

That covers the prioritization of your vendor debts.

Now we will list out all the other debts. These are the loans, the leases, the lines of credit, etc. If you do not make payments on these items, the bank will initiate actions to retrieve the collateral. We will discuss how to deal with these obligations below, but let us prioritize this list before we do so.

First consider the loans or debts you have signed for *personally*. These will be the priority 1s for this list. The reasoning is as follows: even though you have technically incurred this obligation as a business debt, you are legally on the hook on a personal level, and we want to ensure you are not setting aside those debts, thinking they cannot affect your business.

You will need to take a different approach with those creditors to address these obligations properly. Since you guaranteed them personally, when you are talking with those creditors, different types of questions will arise in the conversation. After you identify whether you have signed personally for the debt or not, look at the others on the list, and in the remarks section at the end of your worksheet, make notes such as:

"This is the lease with the fleet of vehicles and we need the vehicles to operate the business."

Write notes about each of the debts. Things like: "if I don't pay that particular creditor and they come in and take all of their equipment back, then I would not be able to operate."

You may be thinking, "Every single one of these creditors could interrupt my business." This may be true, but you have to set a priority on those you need to deal with first, or those that could shut you down right away if you do not pay.

Which equipment could you lose and still be able to run your business?

Put these lower on the priority list. You will discover that it is not necessarily the largest creditor that gets more of your attention during the debt negotiation process.

Again, consider each debt line-by-line, and add remarks for each one. This will help you define your priorities and determine the best approach to use for each.

After you have set a priority for each debt, merge lists. This will be the master list of all your debts. For each creditor, write down (1) a phone number, (2) an address, and (3) the name of a contact person for that business. Assure yourself that the master list is complete and that you have the name of every creditor. Now go through the list and choose the one you are going to contact first.

Some creditors may have a policy requiring you to pay 100% of the delivered invoice amount plus 10% of the total outstanding account balance. If your current balance with that creditor is $50,000 and the delivered invoice amount is $6,000 you would have to pay $11,000 ($6,000 for today's delivery plus $5,000 against the overall debt) to get the delivery and keep operating.

But suppose for the sake of argument that you do not have the extra ten percent to give because you are really deeply in trouble.

What can you do?

You can negotiate with the creditor. But before you contact them, we can assure you—and we have learned this from 20 years of experience—that unless you have a deep understanding of your current financial situation and the particular approach required for this creditor, you really don't know what to tell them and you do not want to call them until you do.

If you call them now, you will probably end up saying exactly the same thing that all of their other debtors say, and this will get you nowhere.

Developing Your "Story"

Before you contact them, put together all the reasons you are in financial trouble, all the reasons you are in this turnaround situation—it might be that sales are down, or you might be delinquent with some bank loans and the bank is threatening repossession of assets, or a creditor is threatening with a lawsuit.

Write all of these reasons down while asking yourself the following questions:

- *Does the business owe money to the IRS?*
- *How much does it owe to all the creditors?*
- *Does it owe money to the bank?*
- *Is it in default now and what is the status of the business?*

Contacting your creditor and talking with them is the best approach, and here's why: there are many debtors out there like you who owe them money, and these debtors usually ignore the problem rather than being up front with the creditor. They are silent while you are contacting them directly. For this reason, they will view you in a more positive light.

Although we say that you will organize all your

records and then call this creditor and that agency or this attorney, in reality you may already be receiving calls from attorneys or collection agencies. You may not be initiating the calls but rather receiving them. So you will have to look at the approach we are outlining and adjust it to your situation.

We do know this method works and our results—after more than 20 years implementing it—show that you will reduce your overall commercial debt burden by more than 60% on average.

We can also tell you that many people are not comfortable performing this process themselves. You can retain a professional debt negotiation expert to assist you. You can always contact us if you need assistance finding a good one. Our contact information is located in this publication.

Negotiating With Creditors

If the first creditor you address is "XYZ Company," and "Mr. Jones" is the president of XYZ Company. When you contact XYZ Company, you should say something like this:

"Listen, I have a problem with paying my debt, and I would like to put together a proposal. I would like for you to bear with me for a short time until I can resolve the problem. I am going to put together a proposal so that I can make you an offer to settle this account."

And you should be saying this to Mr. Jones, the president (or the owner) of XYZ Company, not a clerk or other low level person you may deal with on a day-in-day-out basis. You need to go directly to the highest individual that you can reach, especially if they are not a public company.

You may have access to the controller; you may have access to the accountant; you may have access to the chief financial officer or the business owner himself. You need to speak with them directly to explain your situation: why you are behind with the accounts payable, and that you would like to send them a proposal by next week.

Let's say Monday at 5 o'clock next week you would like to send them the proposal. Give yourself seven calendar days to put together your proposal. That does two things: first, it shows that you are serious about addressing the problem, and second, it gives you a deadline to do what you said you will do.

You have to meet this deadline. If you say you are going to call them back, call them back at the specified time. If you say you are going to send them a proposal, write the proposal and send it to them.

Also ask them how they would like to receive the proposal. You could offer to send it by fax. If you do, ask, "Can I have your fax number, please?" You can offer to send it by email. If you do, ask, "Can I have your email address, please?" You can offer to send it by mail. If you do, ask, "Can I have the mailing address you would like me to send it to, please?" Put an emphasis on being polite.

And finally, thank them and tell them they can expect a proposal in the next week.

Sometimes a creditor might ask, "Why do you need to give me an offer? You owe me the money, right? Why not just pay it?"

At this point you could say, "I understand that, but I do

have many creditors right now, and I am trying to work out this situation."

You might be facing a bankruptcy, and although you may be optimistic about the outcome, you don't know for sure how the situation will unfold. What you do know is that you will understand everything better next week, so you are going to send them a proposal. Whatever they say, respond with something like this:

"What I would like to do at this time is put a proposal together. I have to meet with my financial advisers and accountant to see what can be done, and I will get back to you within a week."

Also mention that if you are finished with the proposal before next week, you will contact them and let them know that you are sending it so they can expect it. Try to end the conversation there.

Don't go into more detail in the first conversation, but do get back to them by the deadline you specify. It is very important that they realize that you are going to do it and that you build the expectation that something is coming.

Negotiating With Collection Agencies

The approach when contacting collection agencies is similar, but instead of *initiating* a phone call to the creditor, you are *receiving* a phone call from a collection agency or a letter from a collection agency. The collection agency charges anywhere from 30% to 50% of the face value of the amount you owe.

Although a collection agency has no more power than the creditor does, they are persistent. They will harass you and they will do whatever they think is necessary to collect.

And this harassment can be a big disruption to your business, or to you personally. But remember, under the Fair Debt Collection Practices Act (FDCPA), there are a few things you can do to protect yourself. One is to ask them in writing not to communicate with you by phone, and in most states in the USA they cannot call you after that. If they continue calling after they receive the letter, you can complain to the proper department in your state or to the Attorney General.

After you notify them that you want them to communicate only by mail, they will send you a notice in writing that contains the amount of money you owe to their client. Then you move into the stage we call "putting together the proposal." At this stage, you call the collection agency and tell them that within a week you will be sending a proposal to *all the creditors* (emphasize these words).

They may respond with something like, "Well, what do you mean, *all the creditors*?"

Tell them you have more than one creditor, but the proposal you are going to send to that particular agency is going to be the proposal for the agency that represents Mr. Jones, XYZ Company. Reiterate that you have to deal with *all your creditors* right now and that you have a situation that is very complicated. Go on to say that financially it is very difficult for your business with the downturn in the economy and you are currently in a turnaround process and hopefully things will go well.

You can get into more detail about the problems that got you into a turnover situation, maybe that you had to lay off some staff, that the sales are way down, that you are having difficulty collecting your own receivables, maybe that you owe money to the IRS and the IRS is giving you a hard time—all the reasons you have put together in the prior section, the notations on the master debt list. You will use those notes here at this stage in the process.

Tell them the following:

- You are contacting them so you can talk with them
- You will be putting a proposal together within the next seven days
- You would like to confirm how they would like to have the proposal sent—by mail, fax or special delivery.

Let them know that you are currently meeting with your turnaround team, and you are all working together to put the proposal together. You want to stop the conversation at that point. You are basically letting them know that you are working on it and there is hope at the end of the tunnel here.

Again, collection agencies do not get paid unless they collect, so it is important to establish that there is hope for a successful resolution and payment.

Some collection agencies work with attorneys that specialize in the collection process. They may inform you that they gave you an opportunity and you did not settle the debt, so they are referring the account to their legal department. In reality, they can only keep *calling* you or *writing* you, all the while hoping that you are going to finally pay the money because you are burdened by all of their calls or letters and you can't bear this situation any longer.

One thing we can emphasize about the process is that whomever you are dealing with will appreciate that you are interacting with them and not ignoring them. Be in touch with the creditor or with the collection agency, and make sure you do what you say you are going to do. Put a proposal together that will follow the format we are presenting here, and the process should move in the right direction for you.

Negotiating With Attorneys

Negotiating with attorneys is a slightly different scenario. When you get the initial call from them, it may not come from an attorney, per se; rather, it may originate from what we call a "collection attorney," which is an attorney who works closely with a collection agency, possibly in the same office. You may also get a call from a paralegal that works for an attorney.

Whatever the case may be, you need to respond to them. Our recommendation is to contact them and follow the same steps we have outlined in the previous two sections. Whoever calls, the paralegal, the collection attorney, or the attorney, tell this person about your "story."

Let this person know you are putting together a proposal and that you have many creditors; perhaps that you have an IRS problem; perhaps that you have the bank knocking at the door right now and moving forward with seizing your assets. That you are in the middle of a turn-around procedure and you are working your hardest to resolve all the issues so you can avoid bankruptcy.

Tell them that (1) you are willing to satisfy the debt at this point, and (2) you intend to put together a proposal by next week. Again, pick a day that is seven calendar days from the date of the conversation, and tell them the proposal is in the process of being constructed.

Ask them how they would like to receive the proposal, by email, fax, or mail. Whatever their answer is, agree to it and let them know you are trying to find an amicable resolution to this situation and that you do not want it to escalate to the next level—meaning that you understand that if you don't comply, or if you don't agree with the fact that you owe money, then most likely it will move on to a lawsuit. Often, you will get a demand letter stating something like:

"We have been retained by our client, Mr. Jones of XYZ Company, and you have a debt to Mr. Jones in the amount of $50,000, and you have ten days to send to this law firm a certified bank draft in the full amount, and failure to do so may prompt a lawsuit to secure this debt."

The letter has no more power than one you might receive from a collection agency, or one you might get from a creditor, except now it is in the hands of a law firm.

One reason the creditor (Mr. Jones) is using an attorney is because he expects a lawsuit will make you pay. If you receive a letter like this and you ignore it, you might get a second demand letter or possibly you will then get a visit by a deputy sheriff or bailiff or someone who will serve you the lawsuit papers.

Let us finish this section by reiterating that you should not ignore an attorney or anyone during this process.

Instead, contact them and briefly discuss your situation. Tell them you are putting together a proposal and that you are going to be sending the proposal to their office soon.

Negotiating by Mail Versus Fax

For many years, businesses have negotiated contracts and proposals using the telephone or mail or some combination. This is fine if there is no sense of urgency to reach a quick decision.

And while telephone negotiations are typically memorialized in writing for all parties concerned, it takes time to write up agreements, contracts, etc. It also takes time to make copies available to all of the parties by using US Mail.

That is why courier delivery services such as Fed-Ex, DHL and others have proliferated. They are a viable alternative to regular mail service. Delivering documents through a courier service can be timelier, and delivery times are often guaranteed. However, let's explore a better method for negotiating with your creditors and presenting the needed documents to the parties in a timely fashion. You might still want to call your creditors as mentioned in a previous chapter, but you now have an alternative method of communicating.

We have found the facsimile (fax) machine to be a very successful method of initiating the negotiation process. Fax machines have changed the landscape and the time required to effectively communicate printed information between people and businesses.

Some readers may ask, "What about email?"

Our answer to you is that email is also a good method, but you might not have the email address of the business owner, and unless you have a scanner, you may find it difficult to send a signed settlement letter to your creditor or their representative.

Elements of the Settlement Letter

Part 1: The Introduction

This communication will serve as a *formal notice* to your creditor, or their representative, that you will be representing yourself in these negotiations. It is important that you advise the attorney or collection agency of this fact.

Part 2: Stating The Problem

Begin by making a concise statement of the problem(s) you are facing. If you have experienced several financial setbacks, now is the time to convey this to the creditor, the attorney, or the collection agency.

If you have suffered financially due to extenuating circumstances such as employee embezzlement or theft, mention it at this location in the proposal.

If you find yourself in the position of being delinquent in paying this creditor because a customer has gone out of business and owes you a large sum of money that is uncollectible, inform them now.

Also, request a stay of further action while settlement negotiations are ongoing. If legal actions have been initiated, this is a request for an extension of time for you to respond to the summons (lawsuit) if you have received one.

Also detail other actions pending against your company. The letter may also suggest that there are potential federal or state tax liabilities that may render all settlement negotiations and payments null and void at any time.

The possibility also exists that you may be forced to exercise other legal options (meaning bankruptcy). Therefore, time is of the essence.

The goal here is to paint a bleak picture of your financial position. Convey that if you are forced to "exercise other legal options," the result will serve no purpose to any of the parties. In such an event, the creditor will have to wait a significant period of time (possibly one to two years in some venues) while going through legal proceedings, and usually they will end up getting nothing. It makes more sense for them to consider negotiating and putting this matter behind them so they can concentrate on the positive aspects for a brighter future.

This element of the settlement letter is crucial because attorneys and collection agencies handle hundreds, if not thousands of cases. They may not be concerned with the personal issues you are facing.

It helps all parties to better understand how the problem(s) developed, so elaborate where necessary. Also, by providing a more detailed analysis of these problems, they may realize it is going to be more difficult than they had anticipated to collect the money from you. This can be very helpful in the negotiations.

Remember, you are not necessarily a bad credit risk. Many prudent business owners find themselves in un-expected situations from time to time. By stating the problem and analyzing the circumstances that created the problem, it provides a better understanding of the situation and also serves to set up the next element of your proposal—personalizing the problem.

Part 3: Personalizing the Problem

This element of the settlement letter allows you to "humanize" your plight. This is where the "storytelling" aspect of the settlement negotiations comes into play. This section will be the "setup" to provide a solution to the problem(s) you are facing, as well as a justification for considering accepting the settlement offer. Therefore, the importance of this aspect of the settlement letter cannot be overstated and should be addressed with keen interest.

It is important to realize that negotiating directly with a creditor can be very different than negotiating with attorneys or collection agencies. When one business owner (the debtor) negotiates directly with another business owner (the creditor), the creditor may have a more personal understanding or sympathy to the situation. In fact, the creditor may indicate that they have experienced similar accounts payable problems at some point in the past. As such, the negotiations may be more congenial and personal.

Business owners usually have a personal awareness and understanding of the intrinsic value associated with "sweat equity," "goodwill," and other aspects of their business that make it personal to them and their customers. In other words, business owners have a more personal feeling about their business and may be more compassionate when it comes time to negotiate a settlement. Obviously, these negotiations may proceed more smoothly.

On the other hand, when one negotiates on the telephone with attorneys, collection agencies, or collection attorneys, one may experience an impersonal, or even rude attitude. Do not take this personally. The reasons for this behavior are varied but can be reduced or even eliminated by negotiating in written form.

When one negotiates with a general practice attorney representing a creditor, they are typically motivated to get the file "off their desk." If a relatively minor amount of money is owed to the creditor, the attorney may not wish to invest a lot of time on the case since the fees will be nominal or non-existent. Many general practice attorneys have indicated that they are handling this case for their client because they represent the client's other business interests and the attorney may be doing this task as "a favor" to their client, but would otherwise not be doing it.

In this scenario the attorney may indicate that if a reasonable settlement can be achieved, they would be willing to present it to their client. They may even advise the creditor to seriously consider the Settlement Proposal. This is especially true if the consultant representing the debtor has properly set the stage to reflect the debtor's deteriorating position. In effect, if you can "sell the settlement" to the attorney, the attorney will probably "sell it" to their client.

In essence, the attorney may wish to dispose of this matter in order to concentrate on one of the larger cases currently on their desk. Remember, it is not uncommon for an established attorney to be working dozens of cases at any given time. As such, common sense dictates that the attorney may seek to resolve this particular case so they can concentrate on larger cases, wherein the attorney can derive larger fees. If an attorney invests two hours on a small case to earn a fee of say $500, or could invest the same amount of time on a much larger case where the fee may be $5,000, on which case would the attorney prefer to invest their time? We think the answer is obvious: he would invest time for the larger fee.

However, if one finds they are negotiating with a collection agency or collection attorney, the negotiating environment can be quite different. One may experience an impersonal or less-than-flexible attitude.

One of the reasons this climate exists is that the collection agency or collection attorney has a vested interest in collecting as much as they possibly can for their client since the agency or attorney is contingency-based. In other words, the attorney or agency will be collecting a fee based on the recovery amount, and it is not uncommon for these entities to earn fees of 35% to 50% of the amount collected. So, do not take it personally if one experiences a less-than cooperative environment if one is negotiating on the telephone.

By initiating the negotiation process via written communication using a normal and acceptable standard, the process can proceed smoothly with little or no discussion. This written format reduces or even eliminates the personalities typically realized in telephone negotiations. Collection attorneys and agencies are creatures of habit and procedure.

By submitting a proposal in writing that appears to be a standard settlement letter, this reflects a financially desperate debtor who may not be able to keep his doors open, yet wants to try to "do the right thing" towards the creditor by paying as much as possible (as a matter of character). These entities are not as motivated to put a lot of time into this particular collection account. Obviously, if the collection attorney or agency cannot realize a large fee, they will take a small fee and dispose of the case. It is clearly an issue of time management relative to the fee they earn.

In order to "sell the story" your position must present the *personal* side of your dilemma. This may seem contradictory to an earlier statement that collection attorneys and agencies have no feelings and do not care about your problems. They are only interested in collecting the highest possible amount owed since their fee is going to be larger and that is how they make their money.

Yet part of "selling your story" is indicating that while the debtor is faced with overwhelming financial conditions, you also indicated that you realize a certain responsibility in this matter. Further, you want to "do the right thing" by paying as much as possible to avoid making a bad situation worse.

Keep in mind, that many creditors do not want to face the prospect of chasing you through a year or two of bankruptcy court, only to collect nothing. You might not be thinking of going through bankruptcy, but we have used it many times to make a point with a creditor and their fear alone does in fact work. As the old saying goes, "Part of a loaf is sometimes better than no loaf at all."

When a settlement letter suggests that you "feel badly" about what has occurred, that you want to do the right thing, and that you are attempting to act responsibly to resolve the matter to the best of your ability, in essence, you are *apologizing*. This tends to personalize or humanize the situation.

So, this part of the settlement letter is extremely important as it may accomplish the following:

- Suggests an admission to a certain responsibility in this matter
- Offers a perceived apology by you
- Suggests that an out-of-court settlement is desired
- Suggests exploring options to resolve the matter
- Sets the tone for justifying considering the settlement offer

By presenting these elements properly, in portraying a desperate yet apologetic climate on your part, one should find that in many cases the settlement offer will be accepted, signed and returned by fax within twenty-four hours. If the tone of these elements of the letter is proper and the subsequent offer makes sense, it will be easy for the creditor, or their representative, to justify accepting the offer, thus putting this matter behind all parties involved.

Part 4: The Solution (or Offer)

In presenting the previous three elements of the settlement offer, one should have laid a solid foundation for the creditor to consider the offer by outlining the details of your problem(s), admitting a certain obligation & responsibility in the matter(s), and suggesting that "something must be done."

This is the part of the settlement letter where you tell the creditor, or their representative, how you intend to deal with the outstanding creditor claims. For example, you would indicate in the letter that the total number of claimants has been divided into 3, 5, or 10 (whatever works for the situation). The letter should also explain that a financial settlement will be presented to each claimant in each group.

Each claimant shall then have 48 hours to accept or reject the settlement offer. The letter states that: "Should an offer be rejected by a claimant, that claim shall not be reviewed again until all claimants, in all claimant groups, have responded to the settlement offer."

The letter will then state that any potential for second-round offers will be on a first-come, first-served basis, assuming funds remain available for a settlement. Please understand that if you only have one creditor, this will not be applicable.

The psychological impact of the entire letter is elicited in this portion of the fax to the creditor. One has just outlined that the amount of money owed to the existing number of creditors far exceeds your ability to honor such debts. However, in an attempt to "do the right thing," a scenario has been devised to provide some payment to as many creditors as possible.

Most importantly, a sense of urgency has been established, implying that only a short window-of-opportunity exists for the claimants since the funds available for settlement will be exhausted soon, especially once your position becomes public.

SPECIAL NOTE: our experience is that when your position becomes public to your vendors, suppliers, bankers and competitors, every creditor will want to get what they can from this "fire sale" before funds are no longer available. This sets the stage for settlement.

When appropriate, some of the following solutions should be inserted in the settlement letter:

- A straight, one-time payment with reduction of amount owed, plus any accrued costs, fees or interest.

- Survival payments provided to allow you to remain active, as an ongoing, viable concern, perhaps while bridge financing or accounts receivable factoring is arranged.

- Graduated workout payments to continue the business relationship between you and the creditor. This option may allow the creditor to recover some or all of their costs over a period of time, if the creditor agrees to continue the relationship, even if on a cash-only basis.

- Schedule monthly payments, perhaps with a balloon payment at the beginning or end of the settlement terms.

Properly and professionally worded settlement offers typically receive the most expeditious responses. One may even combine elements to continue providing to the creditor reasons to accept the offer. Suppose the letter has outlined the desperate financial situation facing you.

You must determine the most appropriate settlement that allows you to keep your doors open, or whatever the goal is. Let's also say that you want to provide additional food for thought that may cause the creditor to accept the offer. The following might serve as an example of how one could word and present the offer:

> "In light of the aforementioned consider-ations as to my financial conditions, XYZ Company wishes to tender a settlement offer of $2,375.00, as a payment in full. This payment is offered as a survival payment that may allow me to continue to operate our business, even if at reduced production levels. Settlement payments to claimants in group 1 shall be remitted via cashier's check within seventy-two (72) hours of acceptance. This offer shall be held open as a "priority account" until the close of business on Wednesday, May 20, 2009. A faxed response to our office will expedite dedication and payment of funds to accepting claimants."

Another facet to consider in presenting the settlement offer is to provide options. Often it may be desirable to make a settlement offer based on a one-time payment to resolve the matter, with an alternative, perhaps indi-cating that a higher amount can be paid if done so in monthly payments.

In other words, one may wish to present two offers in this portion of the settlement letter. One may indicate that a one-time payment of $2,500.00 could be viable or payments of $250.00 per month for 13 months ($3,250.00).

The beauty in presenting either/or offers is that both options to resolve the matter work to your benefit. Either/or offers provide for a win-win situation because acceptance of either of the options is beneficial to you.

This is professional language that speaks logically, yet softly. Properly offered, a settlement letter also allows the creditor's representative to accept less than the total amount owed, without the creditor losing face or feeling that insult has been added to injury in this matter.

Historically, these professionally presented offers are more readily accepted. If the offer is not accepted, the door is still open to continue negotiating.

Part 5: Justify the Offer

You might believe that negotiating by telephone will convince the creditor to accept an offer. This method typically requires you to go "back and forth" in an attempt to reach a settlement agreement with the creditor.

While "begging" and "sniveling" may come into play on occasion, experience has shown that using the Settlement Proposal reduces or eliminates the need for such activity. It is also more professional and allows for much quicker closing of the case.

To motivate and provide justification for the creditor (or their representative) to consider accepting a financial settlement of their claim, it is best to appeal to their value of common sense and to their ego, and one of the best ways to set up this justification is to provide the appearance that you are (1) not only feeling badly about the situation with your creditors, but also that you are (2) genuinely trying to resolve your debt, and (3) offering a sincere apology.

When we have worked on behalf of debtors, we commonly read or hear the phrase: "my client prays for understanding and forgiveness in this matter and seeks to remedy the situation with an offer of settlement."

Another such expression of similar meaning might be: "My client realizes a certain obligation in this matter. Further, my client prays for understanding and forgiveness of a portion of this debt and seeks an amicable, out-of-court settlement." This is appealing to their ego.

In effect you are offering an apology for the problem(s) and you are genuinely trying to find a way to resolve the problem(s). You are also asking for understanding and forgiveness and are seeking a second chance to save your business and maintain some semblance of credit-worthiness.

Creditors will give a second chance to people who want to receive a credit card or buy a new car, even after they have filed for bankruptcy.

Remember, attorneys love to follow specific procedures and language. One who can communicate to an attorney or collection agency in a manner normal and customary to them should find that settlement negotiations proceed on a timely and predictable course with few bumps in the road.

The other characteristic that should be included in this portion of a settlement letter is *common sense*. By "sharing" information and insights based on experience and common sense, rather than *nonsense*, people have a tendency to read settlement offers very carefully and thoughtfully.

The person reading the letter will likely also ask themselves: "Does this make sense or is this scrap?"

The Settlement Proposal typically suggests that they are dealing with a business in grave financial difficulty. A settlement letter might also imply that the longer negotiations continue, the less satisfactory the settlement(s) tend to be, especially after the rest of the creditors hear about "the fire sale" over at "XYZ Company".

You might have only 1 creditor but if you have a few this would apply to you.

The implication here is that if you and the creditor (or their representative) become involved in a long process of negotiation, you only serve the creditor an injustice. Remember, an earlier portion of the letter indicated a timely acceptance, or rejection of the offer would be in order.

This is due to the fact that only a small financial reserve remains to resolve the debt. This reserve will obviously be depleted quickly once the first-round offers are presented and accepted by other creditors.

Who knows how much will remain in the reserve account after first-round acceptances? Properly presented, this line of thinking causes creditors to ponder the issue very carefully in a limited amount of time. This reminds us of an old New England saying:

"When the gettin' is good, GET!"

In other words, get what you can, when you can, and before it's all gone. Or perhaps, "He who hesitates is lost" might be applicable. So keep in mind, when presenting an offer to resolve your problem, avoid the take-it-or-leave-it approach. This only creates resistance.

When presenting an offer, do so in a manner that conveys feelings, apologies and solutions. One must also take care to give the creditor reasons to accept the offer based on common sense, even if it isn't the exact offer expected by the creditor. The letter must include a reason for the creditor to buy the offer!

8

Business Turnaround Methods

Successful Turnaround – A Definition

What does *"successful turnaround"* mean?

There are many ways to measure and define a successful turnaround. You might say that keeping your business alive for at least one year means that you have executed a successful turnaround. You might say that keeping it alive for five years is the definition. You might say that converting your business from a unprofitable to a profitable company is the definition. Or you might say it is something else. We are going to define what we consider a successful turnaround.

A successful turnaround has two elements:

1. Your business has a *positive* cash flow
2. Your business is transformed to sustain a *positive* cash flow

We believe you could reasonably add a third element

to the above definition:

3. Your business has a well-defined plan to restructure and further stabilize

We think this last item reflects that it is not enough just to fix a few problems with the business and nudge your company back into positive cash flow territory. The fixes you implement to accomplish this may be only temporary; as a result, your company may inadvertently fall back into turnaround mode. Therefore, further steps are necessary.

If—in addition to correcting your immediate problems and sustaining a short-term positive cash flow—you restructure your company according to sound turnaround principles, you will be on the right track to stabilizing your business and avoiding the need for a future turnaround.

The primary approach during this restructuring period is to develop a plan that will identify the core business revenue streams that you can focus on to get your company through this difficult period. Your plan will pare back all unnecessary operations and leave only the core positive cash flow functions of the business. Then you will build back up to a stable position.

Create a Core Turnaround Team

Although you probably have the skills to implement a successful turnaround yourself, it is a good idea to seek some amount of help. This help can include any of the following professionals:

- Turnaround expert
- Certified Public Accountant

- Attorney

Although you may have accounting or legal expertise within your organization, we recommend that you consider hiring experts who are *external* to your organization. This will eliminate any conflicts your own personnel may have with the turnaround process. For example, your accounting department may deserve some of the blame for your current predicament, and they may be motivated to cover this up. This would clearly be an internal conflict.

You can include your controller or your C-level accounting manager on your team, but it is best that the external expertise is available and you will not be solely reliant on someone who may be partially responsible for the problems causing the need for the turnaround in the first place.

The other reason you should seriously consider outside help is because it is likely that you do not have a certified accountant working within your organization, or one with experience working on a company turnaround, or an attorney familiar with the unique issues associated with the turnaround process.

We are not suggesting that you hire all three individuals. You may be able to accomplish your goals with an attorney who is also a CPA and has experience with turnarounds.

Another reason to retain external assistance is because it will help off-load some of the extreme emotional (and physical, time-wise) burden associated with a turnaround. Remember, people will likely be losing their jobs as part of the restructuring, and futures will be changing.

Terminations can be highly stressful, and it will help if you can redirect some amount of the burden of this responsibility to an external source.

It is often easier (at a minimum, politically) to have some external person onsite, a turnaround expert for example, who can act as the focal point during the turnaround process. Besides helping to carry some of the emotional burden, he or she will also help by carrying some of the blame for the difficult decisions that will take place during the turnaround.

This can be a turnaround consultant who comes to your site physically, or it can be simply a coach who will help guide you through the process from a remote location.

A turnaround expert will also help to *diffuse* the process and remove the emotions from these difficult situations. They will help you remember that these are changes that must take place in order for your company to survive.

In the days ahead, you will likely cut your expenses drastically. This translates to significant operational changes, and usually it means you have to terminate jobs. Being a focal point, this external turnaround expert can help shoulder some of the stress and ill will associated with that difficult task.

Sometimes the situations associated with a turnaround can be so emotionally charged that you will have a difficult time seeing the situation for what it really is. This person will help you do that. They can be a shoulder to lean on, a second opinion, or a sounding board for your ideas.

Since this person is external to the situation, they are impartial and can give you a more accurate assessment than someone internal to your organization.

Turnaround Expert

If you decide to bring in a turnaround expert, you can retain a full-time turnaround expert or you can get part-time help. The spectrum goes from bringing in a turnaround specialist who will spend 40+ hours per week on site helping you with every aspect of the turnaround ...to hiring only a coach who will support you remotely via email, telephone, Skype, or video conference, and by utilizing other forms of electronic communication.

Turnaround Consultant

If you decide to bring in more help than just a remote coach, you can hire a consultant for on-site assistance. Although it will cost more to hire one—$400 per hour and up for a good one—the investment will be worth it if you have a lot of money at risk with the company.

We suggest a combination of local and remote support. Consider hiring a turnaround consultant for five business days on-site at $3,200 per day, or $16,000 for a week to start. Follow this with remote communications.

The initial week will allow them to get a good feel for the situation and the expense will be well worth it because it will significantly improve the quality of the remote communications. Your consultant will have an "organic" understanding about your business and all the people involved.

For both a turnaround coach and a consultant, there

are certain features you should require. First and foremost, this should be a person you feel comfortable with. You should like this person in a way that you can only assess personally. Some people are likeable and others are not. We can't explain exactly how to determine this, but if you feel comfortable with them, that is usually a very good indicator.

As a business leader and entrepreneur, you likely know what we mean. This feature may also have something to do with leadership qualities or charisma or trust, but it is probably the most important characteristic because the last thing you want to do is bring in someone that your employees don't like and have this person irritate the situation worse than it needs to be.

Advanced degrees are nice, but they are hardly the most important credential. Someone who has an MBA or a CPA will certainly be a benefit, but if they have no experience, those degrees will not add up to much.

The turnaround professional you select should therefore have a fair amount of experience with turnarounds (successful ones), and if possible with turnarounds in your business sector. Ideally, this person should be a self-starter and a leader. They should be able to deliver an honest opinion even if it is one you may not want to hear.

C-level experience is necessary, and a good understanding of accounting issues would be a huge benefit. This person must also confirm to you that they believe they can turn your company around if you hire them. They should also have a solid grounding in negotiations, and if possible in debt negotiation.

Ideally, here are the credentials you are seeking in a turnaround expert:

- Personable, likeable, and trustworthy
- Honest and forthright, even when presenting unpopular opinions
- Multiple first-hand experience leading successful turnarounds
- Experience with turnarounds in your business sector
- Solid C-level experience with leadership qualities
- Accounting experience and understanding
- A positive expectation on the outcome of your turnaround
- Negotiation background, preferably debt negotiation
- Firm understanding of and experience with formal project management procedures

Note that although you can differentiate on these requirements when it comes to hiring a coach versus a consultant, and possibly not require as many qualifications from a coach as a consultant. We recommend that you do not do this. Even though a coach will have a lesser involvement than a consultant, he or she will be making judgment decisions and giving advice with just as much of an impact as a consultant will, although remotely.

The very first thing you will do after you retain a turnaround consultant is to schedule a meeting with your management team and announce that you have done so, and indicate that this person will be responsible for the turnaround and will be making the decisions.

This will off-load the responsibility and send a clear message that your role will be somewhat passive during the process. The turnaround consultant will get more of the credit for the difficult changes to come.

If you decide to hire only a coach, then obviously your role will be more visible and this will not be necessary although you should inform them because you can still off-load some responsibility for some of the more difficult decisions.

In addition to the above qualifications, a turnaround professional may also be a member of the Turnaround Management Association (TMA). Here again, education plays an important role, but hands-on experience trumps it by a mile when it comes to a successful turnaround expert.

Turnaround Coach

If you are handling the turnaround yourself, a turn-around coach can be an invaluable resource. A turn-around coach can be located remotely from your location and act as a sounding board for ideas and plans. If you decide to perform the turnaround yourself, a coach can make the difference between success and failure.

The benefits of a turnaround coach are as follows:
- They will be a sounding board for your ideas
- They can help you make difficult decisions
- They will off-load some of the responsibility for difficult decisions
- They can give you leadership from experience

- An inexpensive alternative in comparison to a consultant

To locate a turnaround expert, you can check with your accountant or lawyer (external to your company). You can also check with your banker. Many turnaround consultants find work through bankers. If your bank is a large one, your local banker may be able to locate a turnaround expert by making contacts higher up in his organization.

One caveat, however, if you take this route: banks and turnaround consultants sometimes have a cozy relationship. The consultant may get all his or her work from the bank, so they may ultimately put the bank's interests before yours.

There is often a need for *discretion*, and if this is so in your case, you can always advertise in popular business magazines or hire a top consulting firm to perform a search. For the amount of money at stake, this level of action is justified.

After you assemble a list of qualified turnaround candidates, you will interview each one extensively. Check references carefully. This will be a long-term relationship, so you need to be sure you have the right individual for the job.

Certified Public Accountant

You are going to need a CPA who is external to your organization for the reasons discussed above. Spend the extra time to locate one with turnaround experience. It will pay off in the end.

An experienced CPA can file amended tax returns to obtain cash from time periods when your company was more profitable. A quality CPA will have experience with the IRS on audits and will be able to help negotiate a settlement if you have any issues with unpaid taxes.

Attorney

If your company has serious debt problems, as it likely will if you are in a turnaround situation, a good attorney will help you with these as well as with other turnaround issues like personal assets.

If your turnaround expert has no debt negotiation experience, you may be able to fill that hole with your attorney. Formal procedures exist to address debt negotiation, and they are highly effective. With the right debt negotiation process, you can easily save up to 60% on your outstanding debt burden. For this reason, someone on your core turnaround team should have solid debt negotiation experience.

You are also likely going to be dealing with "zone of insolvency" issues, so an attorney is a must for liability reasons. Ideally, you want to select an attorney with turnaround experience.

Identify the Winners and Losers

After you have your team in place, you will identify the non-core business functions, those that are not profitable or necessary to the core business functions and that are dragging the business down. You will also identify those core functions that are having a positive effect on the business.

- Identify profitable products & services
- Identify core business processes
- Identify non-core business processes
- Identify profitable business sectors
- Identify non-profitable business sectors

The steps you take to accomplish this will depend on the type of business you run.

Product-Oriented Businesses

If your business is *product-oriented*—meaning you derive most of your revenue from the sale and distribution of products—then you will need to identify the core functions based upon the particular products that have a positive effect on your revenues.

First of all, for the average business, this is not going to be a straightforward process. Even if you are not very large, you will discover that most products and services and business functions are interrelated and untangling everything—or just getting adequate drill-down visibility on what is generating the most profit—may be very difficult.

Suppose that one of your hottest products is widget A and you literally sell thousands of them every day. But suppose that you don't make hardly any profit on these widgets. If you go through your product line and eliminate all the products that are not high on the profitability list, thinking this will lower costs and increase profits by allowing you to sell only the best items, you may be in for a rude awakening.

It is possible that you have some big customers that

are very profitable and they order a lot of widget A and a lot of widget B, and you are keeping widget B because it is very profitable. But when you eliminate widget A, this customer quits ordering widget B also.

So the net effect is a big loss. This is why you should consider things from every angle. In actuality, you are in a very dangerous and desperate situation, and you will need to make some drastic changes to survive, so you will likely have to risk losing this type of customer because you will be making *big* cuts and not *delicate* cuts.

We present this scenario to illustrate the difficulty.

Find Profitable Products

You can start by printing a report that shows the sales by product line or something similar. You may have to instruct your database administrator to generate a custom report, but it is likely that a report already exists to show the information you are looking for.

You want to understand what your most profitable products are. You can check with your sales managers to see if the report exists, or you may be aware of all the periodic reports that are available. In any case, you will be searching for the most profitable products.

Suppose you are a safety supply distribution company and you sell 20,000 different products. It is likely that each product will have an average cost stored with it. It is also likely that each product will be selling for different amounts across the company. Even though it is not straightforward to determine the exact amount of profit each product generates, you should be able to take a time period, say a particular month or week, and generate a report that gives some indication—and a ranking—of the profitability of each product you sell.

You want to find the most profitable items in your product database, and remember, for the reasons discussed above this is not an exact science. You are spending the time to identify the top of the list and the bottom of the list. Once you do that you can remove the losers.

This report could identify and sort those products with the highest gross profit or some other differentiating parameter.

Actually *removing* a particular product you have identified as unprofitable is often not a realistic option for various reasons. Sometimes you will want to do that, but another approach is to increase the price of the product such that it moves up into the profitable range.

After you have a list of winners and losers, you will then identify all the business processes or sectors that are required to deliver these winners to the customer.

These processes and sectors—and those employees involved in them—are core to the business and you will retain them. Put these on your core list.

For all those products that fall into the loser category (this may be those that fall under a certain threshold line on your sorted "profitability report"), you can identify all the business processes or sectors that are involved in delivering these losers to the customer.

These processes and sectors—and those employees involved in them—are not core to the business and you will possibly cut them from your business. Put these on your non-core list.

Using the safety supply business for an example again, suppose you have determined that your most profitable items are safety glasses and your least profitable items are fire extinguishers. One of the reasons fire extinguishers are less profitable is because they require a service department technician to inspect and certify every extinguisher before it is delivered.

You have always just assumed the service department is a necessary function of the business because they give classes on customer sites and you have always believed this generates a lot of sales and a good rapport with the customers.

It is time to think seriously about cutting the entire service department and removing fire extinguishers. Although we have not yet discussed the profitable and non-profitable business sectors, you have possibly just discovered one while you were evaluating products.

As with everything, these two areas are interrelated and most of what you will be doing will be complicated in this way. But you have just identified that the service department is getting closer to the chopping block.

Services-Oriented Businesses

A similar logic can be applied to a service-oriented business. You will need to identify those services that are profitable.

In reality, most businesses will have a combination of *both* products and services, so the above exercises will be done for each of these sectors of the business.

Business Processes

Now that we have looked at the various products and services and identified the losers and winners, we will look at the individual processes. For this discussion, consider business processes to be the different functions like Customer Service, Information Systems, Purchasing, Accounting, Sales, Human Resources, and so forth.

You will need to look at each of these and determine which of them can be downsized from the business. At first glance, you might think that you cannot live without a sales force, but in these dire times, maybe you can.

You can almost certainly cut the entire catalog department because the company can live without a catalog for the next few months or until it can be revisited.

You may also consider outsourcing the Customer Service function or having the technical support department pick up those additional calls by increasing the wait time on the incoming customer service lines.

The Information Systems department will likely have to stay. But this will give you an idea of the process you will need to undertake. First of all, make a list of all of these processes. Then, with your turnaround team, go down the list and identify those functions you can delete entirely and those that are core to the business. This process may sound harsh, but your entire business may be at stake so in light of that, it has to be done.

Business Sectors

Now you will analyze the various sectors of the business from a different perspective. Again, we can take the safety supply business as an example. First of all, get a printout showing all the branch offices. Suppose you have 50 offices across the United States. As with the products and services, each branch is going to have a certain level of profitability associated with it. Some may be losing money altogether and you will immediately put these on your non-core list.

Some will be marginal, and you will likely put these on your non-core list also. You may decide to keep only those that produce stellar profits. It all depends on your situation and what guidelines you set. You can get direction from your turnaround team here.

The bottom line in all of this is that your company is not making it and you must rank everything from different perspectives and cut out all those extras that you can no longer continue to operate with. What we are doing is trimming down. Later on in the process we are going to build back up, but we are going to use "muscle" instead of "fat."

From all of this work, you will have identified all those functions, products, services, and business sectors that can be cut, all those that must stay, and what changes those that stay will undergo (to pick up the lost function-ality of the business functions that are going), if any.

The Need For a Plan

The business owner who finds their company in need of a turnaround must take the necessary steps to ensure that the business will succeed after the reorganization has taken place. Both economic and internal changes have likely occurred, and these changes have led to the need for a turnaround.

Making money in the business world requires a successful relationship between two critical components:

- The Business Model
- The Market or Customers

Clearly, this relationship between these two components is no longer working in your business, and if something is not done to get things on track, bankruptcy or total business failure will result.

In order to re-synch the business model with the customers, you will need to first take a fresh look at *both* elements of this relationship, and second, develop a plan to get things back on track. We are going to recommend that you do this in two steps. Given that the company is in dire need of action, the first step will be to salvage everything that can be salvaged. You will need to find those things that are currently working and save those. Conversely you will need to identify those elements of your business that are not working and get rid of those.

In this first step, you are looking for the big-ticket items on both ends of the spectrum. You will then review your business in a more fundamental way to determine how to make long-term core changes that will take your business in the right direction for the future.

Right now, you are more concerned with fixing things to get through this difficult time. Here is an analogy. If you have engine problems while you are on the road, possibly you want to get the car running long enough so you can get it back to the repair shop.

Once in the repair shop, you can make the long-lasting changes, but for now, you just need a way to get it safely from the side of the freeway back to the shop.

A key part of any successful turnaround is to have a well-defined plan. This will help in two ways. First of all, it will allow you to communicate with those important people—business owners, stockholders, and other interested parties—that you are on track for a successful turnaround outcome. Second, it will make you think everything through. Third, it will give you a template to work from.

Although the actions you end up taking may not follow the plan exactly because of changing conditions, at least you will have a well-constructed, *written* plan that will give you some guidelines to work from.

CONCLUSIONS

In the current economic downturn, businesses are still filing for bankruptcy by the thousands each month. Although some indicators have improved, if the US government fails to do a better job of managing public finances, a double-dip recession—with further economic calamity—is a virtual certainty. Many economic experts are predicting this terrible scenario, some are claiming we have already entered it.

In this book we have answered the following question:

What can you do to prepare your business for coming economic calamities?

We have discussed powerful concepts that will help you fortify your business, concepts such as (1) *revenue stability*, which can stabilize the income streams of your company, (2) *commercial debt reduction* methods, which can free up a surprising source of hidden capital, (3) *glo-*

balization techniques, which can increase and diversify your income streams, (4) *human resource utilization* in a global market, which can lead to a low cost supply of highly-skilled workers, (5) *expense reduction methods*, a benefit to any business, and (6) *cutting-edge Internet marketing techniques*, a tremendous opportunity that is all-too-often overlooked by many business leaders.

By implementing these methods, you can prepare your company for future economic turmoil, or you can repair the damage that has already occurred. For some businesses, however, it may be too late already, and the time to prepare has passed; for others, there is still time to take the necessary actions to stabilize the business and prepare for the worst. Those savvy business leaders who take the steps outlined in this book will have the resources to weather the storm of a future recession.

About The Authors

André Larabie

André Larabie, MBA, is a Registered Corporate Coach, a Certified Master Coach, a Certified Business Coach, and an Executive Coach specializing in business turnaround and coaching clients with huge debt problems who are being sued by their Creditors. He is distinguished for his expertise in teaching, coaching, business consulting, commercial debt resolution, training, consumer debt collection, mediation, and arbitration. He has owned and operated two collection agencies, a factoring organization, and a business/management consulting practice in both the USA and Canada.

André has authored many college-level publications in Canada, including the following Doctorate Dissertations: "Starting a Factoring/Financing Company," "The Opening of a Business College," and "The Psychological

Ramifications of Online Education."

He has published over 186 articles and has published the following books:

- *Commercial Debt Negotiation*
- *Business Growth Strategies*
- *Business Turnaround Methods*
- *How To Reach Your Own Personal Financial Freedom*
- *How To Reduce Your Personal Debt And Start Living Debt-Free*
- *Stop Trading Hours for Dollars - How to Build a Successful Coaching and Consulting Practice*
- *Law Of Attraction - The Secret Is In Your Mind*
- *Insider's Guide to Explosive Business Growth*
- *Business Turnaround Coaching*

Mr. Larabie holds the following certifications:

 Certified Business Coach

 Certified Master Coach (CMC)

 Expert Ezine @rticles Author

Dane Kress

Dane Kress is an avid outdoor enthusiast with a passion for education in all industries. He is a certified business advisor with a bachelor's degree in education. The experience he has accumulated through setting up various businesses has helped many in the business world with their ventures.